ONE DAY AT A TIME

An Offering For The Journey To Your Unique Self

QUINN HILL

www.lfbookpublishing.com

One Day At A Time: An Offering For The Journey To Your Unique Self

Copyright © 2023 Quinn Hill
All Rights Reserved. Manufactured in the United States of America.

All rights reserved. No part of this book may be used or reproduced in any capacity without written permission except in the case of brief quotations intended for use in critical articles and reviews.

In the event that you use or enact any of the material in this book, the author and publisher assume no responsibility for your actions.

The publisher, Lightning Fast Book Publishing, assumes no responsibility for any content presented in this book.

Summary: One Day At A Time is a book written to guide individuals to their unique desires and definition, and away from societal definitions and expectations.

ISBN: 979-8-9882743-7-7

FOREWORD

Many of you may not find this type of prose to your liking, and that's okay. I have picked up and peeked at many things, only to leave them where I found them. It is encouraging that you paused and are now reading these few words. Thank you; please enjoy this interlude.

TABLE OF CONTENTS

Foreword iii

SESSION 1: Speaking of Life 1

SESSION 2: Introduction 5

SESSION 3: Speaking of Life – A Beginning 13

SESSION 4: Speaking of Life – What You Recall 19

SESSION 5: Speaking of Life - Imagery 39

SESSION 6: Speaking of Life - Spirituality 49

SESSION 7: Notes of Life Lived – Simple Grace 61

SESSION 8: Notes of Life Lived – Hidden Tears 77

SESSION 9: Notes of Life Lived – Pulse and Flow 87

SESSION 10: Living Life, Finding Grief 99

SESSION 11: Service – Life's Sacrifice 111

SESSION 12: Speaking of Life – Lived 119

SESSION 13: Love, Lived Out Loud 145

SESSION 14: Praise, Simple Praise 173

SESSION 15: Session in Prayer – In Prayer with You 193

SESSION 16: One Last Thing 203

About The Author 209

A Letter to You 211

Afterwords 213

Session 1

SPEAKING OF LIFE

Sessions in the midst of crisis, as my world fails, I cry out, moaning in the night and as the darkness ends, another day, another crisis begins.

In the passing rain, drowning, flooding the moments, washing your regrets, there is no hiding your tears, no excuses of allergies and such. Just knowing that the picture painted of your greatness was painted by someone other than you.

Yesterday always happens after tomorrow has already been lived, and your hopes for today are now memories.

One Day At A Time

Notes and Insights

Speaking of Life

Session 2

INTRODUCTION

Speaking in metaphors is a way of hiding behind the phrases and allowing the listener or reader to determine what is meant. This is done at the risk of misunderstanding, misinterpretation, and complete confusion. But there can be such beauty in the use of the proper metaphor to illustrate a point, to give depth to the picture being drawn or to transport the listener to a place in the mind of the speaker. Used badly, metaphors can simply confuse, cause the point to be completely missed, or worst of all, cause the listener to simply dismiss what is being conveyed and leave the speaker lost with so much unsaid. I try to use metaphors to illustrate, to carry the listener to the scene, and to cause an understanding that may lead to empathy with the narrative being shared. Do I often fail at this? Yes, and on occasion, historically. But, it is the occasions when the metaphors work that the failures are worth the cost.

The daily passion of walking through the wilderness of our minds and our lives often leaves us barren, stripped of the joy given us at the first dawning of the day. Laid barren by the moments stolen by thieves, real and imagined, our passion for life is drained away, and we are lesser for the act of living.

Words are a balm with the ability to bridge the chasm separating us from the simple joy of living. Stolen is our joy in the rhyming that is second nature to living, leaving cynicism to flavor the unrefreshing drink at the end of the day. Should we stop seeking relief in the closely guarded and hidden moments, stop fleeing down pathways covered in the mists of our brokenness, yes, for a time, yes. We should simply rest in the lines of prose called to lift you, freeing your spirit to soar.

Celebrate the words, the passion of the wilderness, embrace and dance the colors, the multi- faceted dreams, and free your imagination. Celebrate the singing of your joy, as the words become images rising to a crescendo that vibrates your soul and gives voice to your laughter, your praise.

Word by word – Let your journey begin.

Introduction

Sessions In

(December 2008, Q. Hill)

Sessions in time, Lost in the moment,
We go in and out, Finding no place in line.

Sessions in space, Finding the beauty,
Seeing joy in motion, Lost in celebrating life.

Sessions in waiting, Second to moment, pausing,
Listening, the quiet overwhelms, Hand held out, seeking, You,
In a season of sharing, we share Sessions in Life.

One Day At A Time

Speaking of Heroes and Not Your Dad
(22 May 1984, Q. Hill)

Speaking of Heroes, Speaking cause no one asked,
I'm on street corners,
Waiting on the city bus, or you,
I'm in unemployment lines,
Waiting on a job when there are none,
I'm waiting on welfare,
Embarrassed and mad,
As among the chairs, you play,
Speaking of heroes, Speaking cause no one asked,
Talking today and not about the past.

I'm in summer's heat and winter's cold,
With aching feet and feeling old,
I'm the angel you hate,
When it's no I say
And yes is the only answer you'll take,
I'm the dustpan and broom,
When like fine crystal you fall and break,
I'm the steps on the stairs upwards you take,
The landing where you rest
And the push at your back when you falter,
Speaking of heroes, Speaking cause no one asked,
And not about comic books or television stars.

Introduction

I'm the beginnings of imagination, And the ender of dreams,
Giving you a dime for cookies and cream,
I'm small, almost in tears,
Because of the choices I make,
"It's your birthday, where would you like to eat?"
I'm on the run and full of lies,
With promises of days to come,
When you cried and asked me of God,
Speaking of heroes, Speaking cause no one asked,
I'm the first and you're the last.

Notes and Insights

Introduction

Session 3

SPEAKING OF LIFE – A BEGINNING

In 1952 in the middle of the Forgotten War, near the beginning of America's involvement in Vietnam and in the midst of the awakening protest against racial inequalities, I was born on a couch in the spare bedroom of Big Mama's house. Unbeknownst to me, I was being introduced into a world perched on the edge of great change, great achievements, unbelievable events, great cultural awakening, and a time when the unthinkable and unthought-of happened. History was being written and forgotten every day. What was normal was under attack with victims from everywhere, not just from next door or down the street, but from Nam, France, and Iowa.

But, none of this mattered to me, for my life from the beginning was its own struggle, and all of the world's happenings seemed so much like a paperback novel drama.

Fast forward to today, and the history is again being rewritten. Somewhere I read that the victor writes the history and the loser whispers truths behind eyes shamed by loss. Not sure which of these I am, but the story is being told with shouts and whispers, so listen closely.

Being born at Big Mama's house was not a big thing. Big Mama's house was a delivery room to many of her grandkids, each born into the comfort and love of Big Mama's arms. The difference was that all of the others had a confirmed beginning, with a clear definition of who did who to bring about them. Not so with me. Not sure if I was unexpected, but my reception was unlike the others in that no one claimed me, except my mother, and she had to. Oh, let's be clear, I was loved and loved deeply. But often when looking back through the lens of years and the clarity of everyday living, you compare what you recall with the things you see and hear. Things heard like, "That is this person's or that person's child." or "His father is…" When heard, it opens the gateway to the void in you of no one saying that about you.

Whose child I am was and still remains a family secret, my not knowing who the man that is my father was. My mother took the information to her grave, as did Big Mama and all the others of that time who may have known. It simply did not appear to be important. At least it was not important to them, at least not enough, to tell a little boy. Days of childhood play are wondrous to recall. Even the worst of times are colored by the hand of God and even though the lines are not always clear, there's joy in the memories recalled. At least there's joy in some of them.

Most of my early years are blurred by the passage of time. Maybe, I should have taken pen to paper when I was younger and the memories fresher. I do recall some things.

Speaking of Life – A Beginning

I remember the dinner table, Mama's family, all gathered, eating. We were there, my older brother and I eating quietly attempting to avoid the notice of the man of the house, our stepfather. To be clear, my brother and I did not have the same father; my brother's father gave him his name. Mine did not. We did share a stepfather who appeared to hate us and often showed us just how much. We were kids without protection, a thousand miles or more from Big Mama's house. Then suddenly in the tense quiet, there was a crash, and my chair and I, a toddler, were on the floor. Food is scattered and drinks are spilled, wetting me. My brother is curled up holding his arm, and my mother is crying waiting on the next blow. Not sure which she was waiting on: hers or his. Strangely, there is silence in my memories, none of the words and only the actions, loud and violent, come through. It is like a silent film, except you are one of the actors, and the scene is real. My stepfather was a big man, and standing over Mama, with me forgotten and in the way, he was huge. But my brother holding his arm, pain twisting his face, stared up at him without a tear or fear on his face. Then he was gone, our stepfather, and there was just my brother and I, with him telling me, "Don't you cry, don't ever cry!"

Shortly after that incident my brother was sent away to Big Mama's house, I think. That is where he and I were mostly sent when it was time, and there was no longer space or need for us with Mama. My brother was there, then simply gone. I recall the hitting interspersed with my Mama's beatings, and crying while listening through the walls. There is a void in me where the happy memories would lay. It is as if the memories were frightened into a secret place, and the way back was destroyed. These are some of my earliest memories that appear accessible through the years.

Reflections

In each of us there exists a door, which for many of us is sealed, tightly locked down. Some of us closed and locked that door ourselves. We were unable to trust whatever is behind it to ourselves or God. For others of us, the door itself is hidden, and the way to it has been destroyed. We are left with emptiness and the knowledge that there is a hidden door. The question is do we seek the door knowing when opened we may be broken by what is released, or do we simply go on accepting the emptiness?

Notes and Insights

One Day At A Time

Session 4

SPEAKING OF LIFE – WHAT YOU RECALL

Born in Big Mama's house during a time of great things happening and great things to come, I wonder if I was a mistake that didn't get corrected or simply erased. I was born and now know that love was present, given as a gift to shield, sustain, and remind me that God loves even the brokenness. I recall Big Mama's house.

Recall the wooden house with the tin roof, with a covered front porch near the end of the dead-end street with bush and tree-filled fields on both sides and behind. Recall the backyard with the chicken coop, garden, and spooky old house where we used to play. Recall the joy of simply not knowing. Recall days of wonder, of growing taller, moments of unrestricted play with brothers, sisters, cousins, and others. Recall Big Mama calling you to dinner, and how good the food was to you. Recall the times when you got in trouble and instead of the beating you deserved, Big Mama said, "this time I'm going to let that go." And, what of the days when Mama came home? Recall the joy of your brother and the love that was shown? Recall, "He will be alright."

One Day At A Time

This was often spoken by an aunt, cousin, or others who were present at my Big Mama's house, especially when we were celebrating the opening of Christmas presents and cards. The spirit was high with laughter and the sound of happiness and joy. There was the smell of food, cakes, pies, dressing, turkey, and other good stuff being prepared for the family dinner. The children and young teens were going outside to play with or use some of the gifts they had received. The sounds were great, and each person present was overcome by the blessings of the day. And again was heard, "He's alright. See he's smiling and playing with the other kids. He's alright."

Too young to fully understand what had happened, the young man, who was the subject of the comments, and from some concern, laughed and ran with the other kids. Seeming to enjoy the fun of simply playing, the child was just one of many. He was noticed only because of the knowledge the folks, many of them his relatives, knew about him. But if anyone had looked closely, they would have noticed he never picked up or played with the other kids' toys or gifts. When the kids played with their cars in the dirt out back, he used the one he made of wood. Not complaining or crying when the children, as children will do, complained or pushed his toy out of the game. Nor did he show the pain when the adults, in the manner of protecting the children from something bad, told him to move out of the way. No harm was meant, and the intent was one of love.

Recall, Big Mama was the image of love to the young man. Everyone loved Big Mama, and she showed love to everyone. But, to her young grandson, she shared an extra touch, a bit more of the cake from the trunk, even allowing him to cry on her breast when they were alone. Because that was the only time he could cry and not be looked at as if he were doing something wrong. Big Mama knew that within him there was a need to release, even though at that time he did not know it. She always knew he would not share his release with anyone else. He had learned to become the subject of jokes and comments and be the target of adults and the kids. She also knew he was not allowed to strike back because if he did, no matter the circumstance, he was in the wrong. Love was found in Big Mama whose spirit was simply beautiful.

Grandmother, mother, all that and the only true beauty in the young man's life at that time. I was, and still am, that young man who still does not know his father or the reason why he was set aside to be different. This is not his story or his Life's walk; it could be anyone's told in an unusual way, told in bits and pieces, with stops and starts to be used, hopefully by someone to rise above or help someone else rise. Love calls out to each of us and reminds us, live each day one day at a time. For tomorrow will always be out of reach and yesterday is forever gone, but today is here to be lived and lived completely with love, care and without fear.

There is a song from long ago, "Grandma's Hands" by Bill Withers. This song is about love unbound, recalling the steadiness of love freely given and available to each of us. This song rings in my heart causing the tears to flow, recalling for me a love missed each day more and more.

The Dancing Melody
(17 November 2011, Q. Hill)

Listening to a melody, breaking my stronghold
A Song by Luther, dancing with his father,
Asking for another chance, to dance again,
My tears, wash, but don't ease my pain,
As I, like you, recall the joy of my father,
For me, a man with no name,
Whose face, unseen, is like clouds in the wind,
Tattered and torn, no need to bother,
Ever changing, there is no image to hold.
Just a sweet melody, for others, not me,
Dancing with my father, is not even a dream
A million times I asked, and million times was told,
Wait, go play, or why you bothering, just go,
No one seemed to know or was willing to sing,
The melody that included me,
And dancing a child's tear wet dream
Leaving them a stranger, masked and old,
Hearing the melody, looking for face they know,
As, again, the choir recalls, their father and dancing.

Fact or fiction, who is to say? These are a few words thrown on paper to bring to life the thoughts, dreams and other things living in my head. Does the possibility exist that it is all made up, yes. But, also, the very real fact remains that any good story, myth, or recalling must contain some semblance of truth. You can either spend your time trying to decide, or you can read it and let the events and stories speak for themselves. After all, is that not part of the pleasure of peeking into someone else life?

Again, I say, "Let your journeys begin word by word."

One Day At A Time

Just Another Rainy Morning
(15 March 2006, Q. Hill)

Just another rainy morning,
Where the clouds of my sins block the light away,
First day's dawning, just another busy day
Where one thing after another won't let me pray,
Just another praise song, sang to hide my fears
So, you won't hear my name or my crystal tears.

Just another nowhere day, I don't want
Shine on, call me, touch me where dreams haunt,
Please, don't let me waste away,
Call me, speak to me, don't turn, not away
I'm in Your closet, in Your shelter, call me
Let your gaze fall, your heart open, your love see,
No, Stop! That noise is me, not nothing. Please?

Just another storm-filled night,
Dream blown hail strikes my panes,
Wind whipped branches seek my name
And again, I cry as the owl calls, Who, Who
Hearing your words, urgent, true,
As crystal tears fall, mine, your love calls,
My heart unfreezes with the day's first dawning.

Speaking of Life – What You Recall

The forever question is how to start. Like many others I have ideas, but end up with starts and stops and getting nowhere except confused. But, at this point we have already begun the journey of this gathering of writings, each one different from the other, each with its own story, each line of prose with its own emotions and responses; tied together to try and create a moment of fantasy that is the reader's alone. So, how to begin, how to select the pieces and the order of each, how to aid the one who enters, acting as a guide to their journeying?

Personally, I love the mystery at the beginning of a piece and approach each as a separate entity, allowing the words to create the atmosphere and to open the door to whatever is called to me by the rhythms and flows. The pieces that follow are a glimpse into the beginning fantasies of images created free.

Dream Dancer

Dream dancer,
Dance my dreams for me,
Weave with your steps a fantasy,
With flights of passion
Raising and falling,
As you leap and land, Set my spirits free.

Dream dancer,
Dance dreams earthy and warm,
Wrapping me as you pirouette
In the movements you take,
Spinning, turning, dipping, gliding, flowing
Until dizzily I explode in a lover's climax.

Dream dancer,
Dancing softly, magnificent and free,
Delicately with your body
Expressing my emotions for me.
Then fading, Dream dancer,
Return my spirit,
Leaving me waiting, poised
For the next dance, the next dream to begin.

Rice Covered Floor
(09 December 2003 (Rewrite 2020), Q. Hill)

Afternoon, Saturday, beneath a steeple high,
Her in satin and lace, veil of purest white,
Young girl, her chosen mate,
Run, laughing, through hand-thrown hail,
Rice falls, scattering, forgotten to the church house floor.

Day darkens, by the steeple door, honeymoon begins
She stands, cotton and tears, so few years
Belly expanded, time near ended,
Young woman (girl), abandoned, her man gone,
Stares, at the rice, tears washing, scattered, covering the floor.

Midnight, Cries of consummation,
Passionate and loving, Soft and giving,
Cries of conception, Painful and despairing,
Now small and demanding,
Unheard, as the steeple sighs, beneath the rice covered floor.

Morning, Sunday, her veil torn, her place chosen,
Under the steeple high,
Young woman, totally elated,
Young mother, belly deflated,
Baby crying, slowly dying,
Life flows, unnoticed, across the rice-covered floor.

One Day At A Time

Noon, the steeple cries, worship begins
Praises go up in rising joy,
Words spoken, celebration, joyous release,
Now, recalls, below, silent and cold,
Unseen, young mother and child,
Like rice, quietly lay beneath the rice-covered floor.

Still I Wonder

(19 April 2020, Q. Hill)

Chilled winds blowing over the wasteland of my love,
Broken landscape, forever changing, the way through, lost,
Ebony tears fall, an ocean full, wetting the empty space,
Drowning the dreams, the hopes of this deserted place,
And, still the echoes of love songs, yours, mine, repeat
Moaning, sound loudly behind the unyielding walls,
Welcomed, again, by the loving smile shining on your face
But, still I wonder, seeking our love, now lost.

In a house of a thousand, thousand rooms, we roam,
Furniture, covered, dusty and old, waits for use,
Ready, like our hearts, to welcome and hold, love,
Pictures, family and friends, overlooked, most forgotten,
Framed memories, emotions, hidden by glass and years gone,
Floors, covered by wandering tracks, and discarded pieces,
Broken, crumbled love tokens, like dried flowers, in a vase,
But, still I wonder, seeking our home, now lost.

One Day At A Time

Crying sky, bright lit, fireworks and such, celebrating us,
Loud crashing joy, star-bursting bright, covering the shattered night,
Noise drowning out, silent tears, cries, questions why, booming,
Drumrolls, pounding our hearts, out of rhythm, unwanted love notes,
Written with vows, words no longer true, on paper, tissue thin,
Stories, told of love's tragedies, copied out of history, repeated,
On pillows, wet with wasted sentences, on sheets, so blue, lying,
But, still I wonder, seeking memories, you, now lost, too soon.

Speaking of Life – What You Recall

Often the inspiration or whatever it is that causes you to want to capture it in prose or statements of rhyme is a surprise. The pieces are created from the need to express that whatever. The words are an attempt to create for whomever the passion, images, and the emotions that simply push, demand to be expressed. Therein lies one of my greatest challenges: how to say what must be said and do so in a manner that the person joining me on the journey can navigate the piece and find for themselves the essence of the story and become immersed in all of its passion.

Night Rose, Passion Rose

(11 October 1984, Q. Hill)

Silhouetted by the evening sun,
You blossom and I sleep, Night Rose.
Kiss me in the beginning darkness,
Rise for me my dreams,
Live with me a fantasy,
The intoxicating sensation of you.

Gentle as the breeze, Your petals caress,
Touch me, Passion Rose, Causing me to speak,
To respond with my dreams, My fantasies alive.

In light reflected and silver,
Love me,
Show me the motions,
Lead me to passion,
And reveal my soul incomplete,
Then, Night Rose,
Guide me painfully upward, breathless,
To satisfaction and dreamless sleep.

Night Rose, Passion Rose,
So soft, so sweet,
Born of the night and sleep,
Live forever, my fantasies complete.

Crystal Tears

(22 May 1985, Q. Hill)

Crystal tears form, glistening,
As rain mists the rising evening
And the sun bids the day goodbye,
While dinner is served in a bag for one
To a person missing and blue.
The resting night awakens
And today becomes yesterday,
Creating a moment of shadows,
Shadows that linger becoming memories happy,
Now past
And tomorrow seems distant and unreal
To a person missing and blue.
Crystal tears fall, dropping,
Collecting in open paper boxes,
As the watching moon listens
And a person missing and blue dreams,
Lost in the cycles of sleep,
Of love and you.
As the closing darkness lightens
And tomorrow becomes today,
Crystal tears fade, drying,
Leaving nothing, but a promise,
For the person missing and blue.

One Day At A Time

Caught up in the everyday living of lives colored by the influences of everything, wanted or not, that brush against you, our imaginings are wounded or simply shoved aside. The impact of this loss is often as abrupt as a person rudely bumping you, or as the one who steps in front of you, without consideration, causing you to stumble, and the encounter is overlaid by the smells of their life, sometimes unwashed, other times over perfumed or made-up of glitz and glamor. The unexpected way life crashes into you is sometimes just rude. But, at other times, the unexpected is beyond belief and leaves you simply in awe. The following piece was forced out of me by just such an occasion. Let me give you some of the back story.

It was on an island in the Pacific Ocean near the eastern South China Sea, and I had just completed an extremely long overnight shift. The work had been filled with lots of drama, both mechanical and human. I was tired and just wanted to get home to my sweet bed. As it would happen, construction on my normal route home caused me to take a path that was unknown to me. As I prepared to turn on to the highway, my mind a mess, I turned to look for oncoming traffic, and there unexpectedly was beauty revealed.

There had been a rainstorm during the night, which was blowing out to sea. In the distance, another of the many islands could be seen, black against rising daylight. There appeared to be a blending the night with clear stars on a black-blue background into a day with the light brightening from fuzzy dark edges to light. On the horizon, there were water spouts, mini water tornados of bright white, dancing over ocean waters of the deepest blue. There was no symphony playing dramatic music rising to an overpowering crescendo, but there should have been. With tears flowing down my cheeks, marveling at the glory of creation,

Speaking of Life – What You Recall

I wrote the piece below on a discarded napkin. It does not begin to capture what I was experiencing, but sometimes you can only accept the limitations of words.

Rare Is the Beauty

Rare is the beauty
That comes to you unexpectedly.
Windblown and sun glazed,
Or sometimes, approaching
Or leaving night,
But of a sudden it's there,
Surprising,
breathtakingly Shocking,
And these words are a farce,
How can they explain
The changing of night into day,
Or, the beauty in the fury of a storm.

Rare is the beauty
That is around you,
Unexpected is the times
When your eyes can see
The beauty that astounds you.
In the midst of it all,
You will stand enthralled
And struggle to see
All the beauty there be.

Rare is the beauty
That comes to you expectedly.

Speaking of Life – What You Recall

Notes and Insights

One Day At A Time

Session 5

Speaking of Life – Imagery

The landscape of topics or items to be covered by lines of prose is as varied as a high desert sunset of my childhood with multi-colored hues surprisingly beautiful in a seemingly stark and barren place. To the unaware, the high desert is only that: a stark, barren and dry place. But if only they would look closer or follow the adventure guide, they would see life, the ever-changing features, and some of the mysteries hidden beneath the harsh sands. At other times, the landscape appears easily mapped. The trails and pathways are known because we have traveled them or ones very similar. There's danger in the familiar paths from our becoming complacent and finding ourselves lost as a sudden wind blows and in the whirlwind our life becomes unknown. Then lost, we grasp for the known and miss the fleeing beauty being shown in the chaotic lines, words freed from an uninhibited mind.

The landscape of the lush and fertile tropics with its rush of abandoned order covering the shape of mountains and valleys with a riot of color and life is both frightening and beautiful. We stand in the cleared places wanting to, but pausing to consider, entering the beckoning unknown. There are paths there, but sight distances are so short, so narrow, so confined that the mysteries seem impossible to find; the sounds from within deepen the beat of your pounding heart. But you know your path leads you there as you look back at the surprising desert you just crossed knowing within the chaos in front of you there is beauty in the lines of prose if you are patient and follow where the words lead.

The multilayered meanings often hidden within lines of prose remain a mystery to many of us as we try and often struggle to follow the writer's guideposts and their unclear pathways. Some pieces have within the rhyme and flow hidden pearls of wisdom, wistfulness, and treasure.

SPEAKING OF LIFE – IMAGERY

The Passing Rain
(21 July 2005, Q. Hill)

Passing rain-washes my tears,
Water weathering the life stones,
As the day fades with my smile
Season after season leaving traces, stillborn,
And my joy erased, replaced,
The facades erode, lost images, faded,
By the life sounds I hear,
But, not the trumpet sounds, or heroes shouts
That tear at the wall I've built,
Crashing against the walls of yesteryears,
My stronghold complete,
Life stones built high, against my shaming fears.
Shaken, now awaken, my rest abruptly ended,
Storms pound, things break, dreams fall,
New day, no joy, no praise, just work and pain,
Dawn raises, an army, the enemy beckons me,
Mumbled words, a prayer or plead,
Word passes, to the wall, life's battle calls,
Alone, does my Lord answer me?
And the passing rain hides my tears, washing me.

ONE DAY AT A TIME

Strong and So Very Alone
(25 March 2011, Q. Hill)

I'm trying to peek behind the fortress walls, Beautiful Woman,
But, you say, Listen, Brother,

My walls defend and protect me,
But oh, how I hate the prisoner they make me.
Walking the halls of my sanctuary,
Listening for sounds other than my own
Hearing only echoes of lives past
And the breaking of crystal tears,
Diamonds surround me with their beauty
And still I am cold
Strong and so very alone.

My gateway stands open, waiting for the entrance,
The coming of my passage to the opening of my heart
And the closing of my fortress, my prison
Seek me, Brother, strong and determined,
For the weak only fail and my walls grow ever taller,
As my patience and allowances grow fewer,
I listen for the music of your steps,
Pausing in my pacing to hear, wind chimes calling,
And my heart responding to the notes,
As again, my gate stands undefended, open

Speaking of Life – Imagery

Awaiting your assault to win through to me,
For I am woman, strong and so very alone.

Love me if you are prepared,
To lose yourself in the hallways of my ways,
Caught by the fragrance of my passion
And overcome by the need of my love,
Love me if you can, brother,
For I am strong and unafraid to be alone.

One Day At A Time

So, What Does This Say
(27 June 2006, Q. Hill)

Frosted window glass hides the crystal views,
Obscuring the whispered comments of the lips we read,
Causing our despair to rise screaming to the future,
And the joys so deeply guarded to dissipate with the winds,
So, what does this say of our love, discussed?

Chilled juices, a paper, shadows of today's news,
Opinions, events, shared to fit our perceived need,
And supposing we are all cosmopolitan, mature,
Glad smiles, close not-friends, props needed to blend in,
So, what does this say of our love, those trusted?

Windshield wipers like secret lies wipe away the clues,
Ice-bound, crushed by the pressure our hearts plead,
Penciled notes, passed hand-to-hand, childish, unsure,
Tear-stained cheeks rose-pedaled scents, happening again,
So, what does this say of our love, joy-filled balloons, busted?

Sunburned fog flees exposing hidden valleys, truths,
Words spill falling helplessly planting unwanted seed,
With increasing weight, dreams sag covered by life's manure,
High-walled maze, lost, but, the scent, of love and friend,
So, what does this say of our love, real or one, lusted?

Speaking of Life – Imagery

Multicolored light, world out of focus, just you,
Breathless beauty, saffron and pink, my heart freed,
Gone, yesterday, lost, tomorrow, only today, so sure,
Whispered comments, shocking your beauty, now it begins,
So, what does this say of our love,
blessed, starlit fantasy, diamond dusted?

Speaking of Images

The image of a man, bowed down by his everyday working, held up by the sweet taste of evenings, and strengthened by children of his blood, is a picture shown in many facets. Each different, each a story itself, each reflecting the man, yet none are complete showing only what we are allowed to see.

The image of a man reflects his loves, his losses, his wins, and all the tears that cover them. He is colored by the work of his hands, his mind, and his loves. The carving, standing in clear relief, shows yesterdays, a million or more, and todays, life one day at a time, all clearly marked by the carver's hand as he shaped the man for tomorrow.

The image of a man is etched with the pain of daily struggles, some small, some large, that are welcomed as the price of the day. Each tear is a moment captured in his mind. A mind that is already overflowing with moments already lived and ones hoped for. Not all pain hurts, some of them taught the man, some of them stopped him; others of them were the pain of love overwhelming. All of them held with love for lessons given and for their being part of yesterday.

The image of a man is incomplete without the love of one who knows what has bowed him down, what each in stark relief said of him, and which of the scars are fresh, still hurting, and which are healed aching only when touched. The background of the image is bright with this love that highlights and frames the man. The image of a man is completed by the love given him without cost.

Notes and Insights

One Day At A Time

Session 6

SPEAKING OF LIFE – SPIRITUALITY

Whether or not you are a person who believes in a Creator, for me I call my Creator, God, Yahweh, or Elohim, we must speak about beliefs. For you the focus of your beliefs may be based on the name and deity that fits and shape your beliefs. Wherever you stand, whoever you do or do not believe in, most of us find ourselves from time to time caught in the grasp of something we do not know or understand. For some this experience is life-changing, for others it is passed off as emotions, illness or happenstance. For others, the experience is attributed to their faith walk and their relationship with their higher power. The experience for them is taken as an encounter with that higher power.

I am called to write about my higher power as the point of reference for experiences beyond my everyday understanding. Words flow on to the paper; the everyday happenings, mundane, and often considered normal are all rewritten by the relationship. Sometimes, the encounter leaves us in awe and seeking more. Sometimes, we are lost in the simple, yet unbelievable, experience of the close encounter with that which is beyond explanation. We simply praise.

I could go on, but lines of prose, written under many conditions, speak for themselves creating for us, the readers, images to match the message intended for you the reader.

Please recall your higher power as I speak often of mine. Please take a moment and listen to what is asked below.

One Question

There on the edge of the high precipice, a beginning or ending, stood a man, simply staring out into the open space before him. Marveling at the awesomeness of God and without thought, he opened his arms and lifted his hands in worship. As he fell into the arms of God, he closed his eyes and leaned forward, as if to take flight.

Well below was a lookout point where people gather to view the incredible sight. One of the people there on the lookout point looked up and saw the man. After a moment, he realized he knew him and became frightened. Scared because he knew the troubles the man was going through and how very depressed he had become, fear filled his heart as he scrambled for his phone and motioned frantically to the other people there on the lookout point. Pointing upward, he said, "I think he's going to jump!" Everyone was now looking up and calling to the man, who did not answer. Soon, the police and other emergency services arrived.

Once they realized the seriousness of the situation, the police acted quickly to get to the top of the ridge line and to the man standing on the edge. Still with his arms outstretched and leaning way forward, the man did not even react to their coming or calling out to him. Finally, one the police officers walked quietly up close to the man and softly, so as not to shock him into jumping, asked, "Are you alright?" The man turned and looked over his shoulder, puzzled, and said, "What?" More urgently the policeman asked, "Are you alright? It's not worth it to jump." Again, but this time looking a bit annoyed, the man turned and asked, "What?" Then leaned even further over the edge and raised his arms even higher. The policeman yelled, "Don't do it! Please, don't do it!" The man slowly lowered his arms, turned, and walked past the policeman, who let out a sigh of relief.

The policeman touched the man's arm to stop him. The policeman asked, "Why were you going to jump?" The man looked at him and laughed, "I wasn't going to jump. I was trying to fly." Now, really worried, the policeman asked, "Are you going to try it again?" The man responded, "No. I asked God for wings, and He told me, "No." The man then walked away with a smile.

Why was he smiling?

One Day At A Time

It Only Matters
(16 April 2013, Q. Hill)

It doesn't matter the day or time,
The offense, real or imagine, or your crime,
It doesn't matter the wishes or greatest hope,
The planned or handed down dreams you broke,
It doesn't matter if it was intended to be,
Or if received just by chance, surprising and free.

It doesn't matter the words spoken
In truth, or as lies, or just as a token,
It doesn't matter who loved you,
Or who you loved, none were so true,
It doesn't matter the tears shed,
Or the life you've led.

It only matters what He said,
His Blood for you freely bled,
There is no hiding from what is true,
Love, cross-held, is all that saved you.

It only matters that for your life,
The whip scourged Him with stripes,
It only matters for you He died,
And for you, He did Rise.

Speaking of Life – Spirituality

It doesn't matter if you believe,
Your sins He did relieve,
It only matters that He gave,
And because of Him you are Saved.

One Day At A Time

Who Touched Me?
(10 Oct 2005, Q. Hill)

Every tear flowed without ceasing,
Washing hopes, dreams, like used tissue, away,
Leaving emptiness, injured hurt, life seeking.
Hopeless, broke, broken, just the grave, waiting,
Slowly filling with yesterdays, tomorrows, mine,
That drowns my todays, leaving me faint, falling.
Then He brushed me, just a caress.
Suddenly, lighter than a feather,
Dreams, mine, float by me, rising, pirouetting,
Dancing, embraced by Hopes long lost, blessed.
Shedding yesterday's darkness, laughter appeared,
Still, my tears flowed without ceasing.

Again. He touched me, just a breath of air.
Light filled, love healed, still I seek,
Who touched me?
Washing my yesterdays, lifting my joy,
Who touched me?
Barely a caress, so gentle it seems, but what power.
Who touched me?
Gold has no value, so priceless this seems.
Who touched me?
Please touch me, touch me, love me again!

SPEAKING OF LIFE – SPIRITUALITY

Face to Face
(2 August 2007, Q. Hill)

Man to man, let's speak,
No innuendos, or stupid codes,
Just say it to my face,
Be a man, not childish or weak,
Don't waste time, I can't afford,
Life is rushing, surprising me,
Got to move, can't stand in place
Livin' hard and I'm cursed,
Tired of waiting on Jesus and God's Grace.

Listen, man, my partner, my "P"
Life's drumbeats pound me,
Rocking the roll, slammin' the street,
Wakin' an answer, the flow in me,
Calling the empty places
Crashing my dreams, disturbing my sleep,
I hear angels sing,
Harmonies rockin' my soul
Opening the curtains hiding my fears,
Showing me curses, new and old,
And the grave, so icy and cold What does God want of me?

One Day At A Time

Brother, I'm not a boy, not weak,
But, the words, burst unstoppable from my mouth,
Prayers, pleas, spoken out loud,
My sins, uncovered, the truth jumping out,
Convicting me, another open and shut case,
Calling me to God, Face to Face,

What answer can I give? For the life, as a man, I live,
Standing broken, bowed by the weight,
My prayers, what good are they,
If when He called I turned away,
Tell me what can I say,
When God calls me Face to Face.

Hold, my brother, if man to man, we speak,
Then recall Calvary's peak
His Life given for your sake, your hurt
No angels singing, no childhood dreamin',
Not just a man, but Holy and Pure,
Who knew the cost of the generation's curse,
Of your daily redeeming
And still opened the way, again and again,
For you to meet God, Face to Face.

Speaking of Life – Spirituality

Sticky, and All That
(06 April 2020, Q. Hill)

Peppermint candy, all sticky and such,
Braids, long, shining and such a mess,
Tall, not too, thin, but not frail,
Or even the least, weak,
Facing the everyday of someone else's
Yesterday, lived through their mistakes,
But, God makes none, He said so,
As He kissed my sticky face.

Taffy, sticky and all that,
Pulled by all, each a different shape,
So busy are they, that they forget the taste,
Not artificial, with sweetener added,
The taste, bitter and sweet, mine
Not theirs, no silly treat, or lost fantasy,
Just, the Truth, as God called me,
As He, wiped my tearful face.

One Day At A Time

Rock candy, hard, sweet, now sour,
Not sticky, unless left out, discarded,
By those unable to take the strong taste,
Frowning, unable to accept the simple grace,
Of the dancer, beautiful and free, soaring,
Gifted and blessed beyond belief,
Broken, yet flawless, as God intended me,
As He, shaped my praising face.

Notes and Insights

One Day At A Time

Session 7

NOTES OF LIFE LIVED – SIMPLE GRACE

I simply love to listen to nature. The peace and aliveness of it is simply glorious. It is why I go hiking. It brings you closer. But I also walk the streets of whatever city I am in for the same reason, to feel life and its flow. Cities are the gathering places of people. All kinds are found there, mixed one to the other, over and over. The people are the ingredients, the streets are the containers, and everyday life in its many varied forms is the mixer. People are the reason for the cross, for the need of a sacrifice beyond measure, and for each of us to follow the example of Simon, who carried Jesus' cross, and bear for a while the weight of someone other than ourselves. Grace, unmerited Grace.

The city streets and many of those lost on them, I was one of them, are part of my penance, which has been placed on me by my life lived. I love the quiet majesty of nature unbound, just knowing it is there aids me when I speak to a child, or young person, or someone on the edge of nowhere. Every day my heart is broken again and again, but my accepting this as part of the cross I bear heals part of the brokenness. And, I would go for a walk.

Not many understand my need to walk the streets, mostly because those streets are worlds away from where they are and where they hope to be. But if you have ever been to that edge and then redeemed, you may be called back to the edge to serve. And, that's me. I answered yes when told to go, to return to my one-time refuge, the streets, and be there, a guidepost from the edge for someone lost and seeking a path, needing help with the cross they bear.

Please know there is no condemnation if this is not part of your penance. Your walk is yours and the crosses you bear are yours, whether you pick them up or not. Sometimes, someone else will be given your cross to carry, especially if for a while you are unable to bear the weight. But, know that as Jesus showed us, your cross is your cross and only you can bear the full weight of it. But unlike Jesus' cross, yours does not carry the sins and the redemption of us all, and even if you do not carry it, Jesus already has picked it up. This is the reason you can be lost, go to the edge of where you end, look into the nowhere and still hear the quiet voice calling you to turn and take the hand of Love without measure.

Simply listen to the voice of nature, the glorious peaceful aliveness of it is often the voice of Love calling you to help someone carry the weight of their cross as yours is being carried by Love without measure. Peace.

Listen

(05 January 2010, Q. Hill)

Storm winds, icy and burning, reach for you,
Your life out of control, lost to the daily winds,
Words, like tears, yours, stripped of their meaning,
Beaten, pressed down, your knees wounded,
And still, the life-changing winds snatch, moments,
Wind-blown echoes, calling man of God, listen.

Church house walls, saints, sinners, alone, you,
Life given, gift lifted, scouring foes and friends
Preached words, fiery/true, deaf to pains' keening,
Hands, uplifted, knees pillowed, ungrounded,
And still, the life-stealing sins roar, torments,
Pew-thrown praises, calling man of God, listen.

Bible pages, brittle and frail, worn nearly through,
Youth gone, life spent praying, now crying again,
Holy Words, comforting, others, world's screaming,
Prostrate, eyes open, knees, scarred, love unbounded,
And still, the life unrepentant speaks, comments,
Last whispered pleas, calling man of God, listen.

One Day At A Time

Quiet times, peaceful and resting, so very few,
You alone, life lived, blessed, one true Friend,
Hearing Words, Well Done, tears streaming,
Standing, not alone, knees healed, unwounded,
And still, the life song, sings, Glory, moment to moment,
Wing-borne prayers, calling man of God, listen, please.

Pain in my heart

Street corners, broken windows, junkies and HOs,
Hustlers, slingers, pimps, thugs, and citizens,
Police, preachers, liars, leeches, and thieves,
Drafted, posted on frontlines of life's desert war zone.
Mamas trying, fathers absent, whining and lying,
Blaming, who, me, you, the ones, mentioned before,
"Knock, knock", anyone there, anyone to love me,
Pain in my heart, gunshot in the dark, lost before I start.

Just met another solid glass door, closed,
Slammed even as I stormed in,
Look at me, demands wasted, everyday pleas,
For my child, for life, wounded, hope gone,
Tired, weak from want, day by day dying,
Broken, again, by your eyes, my lies,
"Knock, knock", landlord, police, you, looking for me,
Pain in my heart, prayer in the dark, offering up my heart?

One Day At A Time

Street corner churches, drunks and liquor stores,
Babies, teens, old and broke, always short, never in,
Politicians, serving you, me, tricks up their sleeves,
Pushing, you, out front, again, from their walls of stone,
Promises, spoken, prayers heard, angels flying,
Confused, must choose, which is true, which the lie,
"Knock, knock", here or there, love or the streets,
Pain in my heart, Jesus did His part, Can I call Him Lord?

Simply Loving
(11 April 2017, Q. Hill)

As my morning prayer ends, my daily sinning begins,
Wrapped in the Joy of a prayer complete, I fall again,
For just beyond Amen, the abyss waits,
And thou, I wear the Armor, in my mind,
There is no escaping the drift of the blowing winds,
As the moments move me away, whisperings begin,
And my joy fades; day becomes bitter to the taste,
That's when the Spirit within seeks and finds,
Sheltering, embracing, simply Loving my Heart.

It's noon, the middle of another difficult day,
Crazy, out of control moments are stealing my praise,
No song of joy, no uplifting, just one burden and another,
Some mine, others delivered, all tearing at the walls,
Walls no longer shielding, no longer strong, just crumbling clay,
And, as the moments escape, on I stumble, blinded and dazed,
My morning's joy faded, the day is a pressure seeking to smother,
That's when the Spirit within seeks and finds,
Sheltering, embracing, simply Loving my Heart.

One Day At A Time

As the day comes to a close, I pray,
Crying from the pain of my sinning, asking for release,
Bowed down, almost broken, at the abyss' edge,
My soul cries out, my heart listens, the silence grows,
And each tear, each moan, melts the day's sins away,
The winds continue to blow, but in my prayer, Peace,
On my knees, bruised and wounded, remembering God's Pledge,
Joy flowered again, fading the day, whispering I Know,
That's when the Spirit within seeks and finds,
Sheltering, embracing, simply Loving my Heart.

Tear Drops Fall
(07 December 2011, Q. Hill)

Teardrops fall
Each a child too soon called
From a world where sin is truth
Where mothers cry as they let loose
And fathers ask, why so young,
As again the steeple's bell is rung.

Teardrops fall, an ocean they fill
Each a hope, unborn and still
Promises, written, spoken out loud
Lost to fear and growing crowd
No longer shouting, or loudly proclaiming,
Anything, speaking but another's shaming.

Tear drops fall, from a cross on high
Forgiveness given with a final cry,
Father, Of those also hanging, said one,
Lord,
The other, like many, said, if you be god…,
And over our shoulder we look to see
If the world, not Him from the cross, pauses, sees me.

One Day At A Time

Tear drops fall, for a life now done
And wondering, again, if you knew the Son
Whose voice called you from the many
Or did you sell Him for nickel or a penny?
Covered with false praise, and unrepented sin
Or blessed, welcomed in?

Reflections

I stand on the edge of a deep divide, a deep gorge. I am impressed by the things I see. I'm impressed by the feelings inside of me. I'm impressed by the surge of excitement that comes through you just looking at the things God has made. The awesomeness and beauty God has given us gives us a perspective of how big our God truly is. We can only offer a thank you for the opportunity to see these things.

Today's A Joy
(05 October 1984, Q. Hill)

Today's the joy,
Uncontrolled, it's free, Just a feeling that's in
And around everything, Especially me.

Steps of dance, Simple pirouettes,
Hugging yourself and turning,
Spinning until you collapse,
Collapse from lightheaded weakness
And still you move,
Move to sounds only you seem to hear.

Hi, Hello,
Good Morning to you.
How are you doing?
The weather?
Sunshine!
How could it be any other way?

The sunrise began it all,
Simply in its complexity,
Overpowering in its beauty,
Leaving you totally breathless
As it opens the day.

Today's a joy.
What else can you say?
Except,
"Thank you GOD
For sending it my way."

Reflections

God has always been part of my life. We were introduced by Big Mama. She took us to church, pinching us when we misbehaved or fell asleep during service. Big Mama and her Bible made God real. Her God appeared to have left when she passed, taking with Him all the love in the world. My God is present, but Lies seeks every day to separate us again. I hold to the lifeline of His Word and to the promises of my Savior, Jesus Christ.

Notes and Insights

One Day At A Time

Session 8

NOTES OF LIFE LIVED – HIDDEN TEARS

When speaking of sessions in life, you must on occasion speak about your own life. We are shaped by the many sessions, the many incidents and encounters and the people we are in contact with. Usually, the most impactful are members of your family and people allowed to be in your life. My older brothers and I were often separated, living with different relatives in different cities with little or no means of contacting each other. There was little or no opportunity to use a telephone; there were no cell phones or multimedia. The manner or reason for our separation was not always known, at least to me. There was often little warning or apparent preparation for the resulting moves of my brothers or me. The impact on each of us was different except in one way, the feeling of abandonment and the accompanying, hidden tears.

Abandonment for me was the feeling of not belonging anywhere and the need to avoid forming relationships. Relationships weaken you allowing others to control, significantly impact you every day, and hurt you in places you were unable to protect. For most of my life I thought I was the only one of us, my brothers and I, who felt this way, abandoned. It was during a conversation at the dinner table when we are all adults and at a point where we each needed to talk, it was said, "I felt abandoned and unable to do anything about it." And it was not me making the statement. I was shocked to hear it. "How could this be true?" I asked. During the resulting conversation, we each shared the sense of loss felt when dropped off at a family member's house or when placed on the Greyhound or in the backseat of someone's car. It came out; we each wondered what we had done wrong to make them no longer want us around. And the other item in each of our telling, other than not letting them see you cry, was why anyone didn't speak up for us.

When no one speaks for you, your imagination creates scenarios to help you deal with what's happening. I know now none of the scenarios I created were true. Mama did not hate or not want me. I wasn't just the "pass around kid" or the "in the way kid". There were hidden agendas and secrets in play that often had nothing to do with me and everything to do with the others, adults, involved. But what does that matter to a child? Those things meant nothing at all. These sessions in life became the foundation of my emotional and relationship life, affecting me even today. The writings contained within this document are some of the results of the one outlet given me: reading. It did not matter the document or what it was written on, I read it. As a child and young teen, cans of soup, bags of flour, road signs, books and magazines of any type or genre, porn included, or anything else with words, were my escapes. Comic books were a special escape with the various heroes, villains, and people coming into their own stories. I found when you lose yourself in the stories or content of the science, math, and history books, the happenings around you have less impact. And when you do, you can remain remote from much of the daily pain.

Libraries and bookstores became my refuge, especially libraries. The books were there and free to read. It also helped during the times when being home was not the place to be that the libraries were either warm or cool depending on the season. Even during the session in my life when the streets were my home, the libraries never refused or abandoned me. I still visit libraries every chance I get in whatever city I find myself. There is a comfort there, a welcoming, and an opening of the entire world through the words waiting to speak.

Not sure what my brothers found to ease their personal pains and feelings of abandonment, or if they did. For me, it was the words, the scenes and imagery, the worlds created and the people waiting to be met. You can become immersed in a story and just relax, letting the gift given you by the writer guide you. No one questions deeply when you shed a tear or two and they see you are reading a book. It is assumed the story has affected you. Often the truth is the story has reached one of your hidden places and the tears it contains. Yes, this document is an attempt for me to not only find healing in the writing but also provide you, the reader, with an opportunity to become immersed and lose yourself for a moment in the lines of prose. At least, that's what is hoped.

Love can be described in so many ways unique to the individual giving the description. There are many things coloring the picture love has drawn in each of us. There's the sweet green of new love growing, the vivid reds of our passions unleashed, the purples shading to blue that we all know, and the yellows tinted throughout by multi-hued browns fading to ice cold whites of love being lost. All colors imaginable, each unique, the many hues of love being lived out loud. I could go on speaking about love and never come close to understanding it. Understanding love and the hell it can cause has plagued men and women forever. And, still we try. Loving again and again in an endless cycle of hurting, denying, crying, accepting, moving on, and seeking love's joy again, we try. For me, love within me is at constant war with the pain within me and pains' anger army of old hurts. Let me explain, please.

My earliest memory of love out of control is of my high chair falling forever to the floor, my older brother crying out in pain, and complete chaos as my mother's husband lost his mind again. Then we were at Big Mama's house. Sweet smells, soft hugging, Big Mama's hands and for a while peace, simply being loved. My love cycles, at least back then, always started with pain or hurt and ended with Big Mama. Then Big Mama died and so, it appeared, did love.

My every day is spent like so many people, seeking love. There are so many opportunities to fall in love, but so few times when love loves you back. Our blindness to the failings of falling in love, and the growing numbness to it, leaves us defenseless to the allure of love. I, like many others, sought love through its physical expressions. Thinking that making love, just having sex, was the way to the heart of it, I sought physical contact every chance I got. But the horrors and pains of my youth were not so easily set aside and soaked through the ironclad walls of my defense, coloring each relationship. The destruction was not just to me, but also to whoever was unknowingly involved in the losing battle. There is not enough "I'm sorry" in the world to make those failings right. So, inside I cry for what may have been and what was forever lost.

When Sundays Are Not Enough
(20 August 2015, Q. Hill)

Heard teardrops striking the open palms
Crystal diamonds lost to the grief of today,
Flowing without end, unseen, unfelt,
Heart-broken, seeking living alms,
Gifts, given, but, unable to raise the joy, this day,
As angels, lift lost love, without my help,
Sundays are just not enough.

Furniture, scattered, stacked high,
Clothes, torn, walked on and dirty,
Toys, no longer new, so out of place,
Whispers, hidden words, as I cry,
Its 8:00, they came at 7:30,
And a door, closed, once ours, we face.
And, Sunday is so far away.

One Day At A Time

Flowers, wilting in an empty vase,
Recall, love, overflowing and new,
Kisses, thrown without care, freely yours,
Passion, hot, love overheated, first taste,
Life, conceived, from me and you,
Now, alone, no answer, no lights, empty doors,
Sunday is not my wedding day.

All night, praying, crying, morning now,
But, the darkness, still in my heart, reigns,
And, calls again, and again, Your name,
As I pause, tired, broken, head bent, a simple bow,
There is the cross, and my name, my pain, He claims,
Then, in the moment, exhausted, I heard, again my name,
And, knew Sundays are never not enough.

Silver Chalice

(18 February 2021, Q. Hill)

Silver Chalice resting on the window sill,
Beauty given as a gift of love,
Or brought to show old or new wealth,
Simply a cup made of precious metal,
Made precious by desire, maybe love,
Sits alone, still part of a set, now gone,
A cup left empty, forgotten in the window light.

Silver Chalice shining, so pretty and bright,
Resting in velvet of the darkest hue, purple or blue,
Lying with others, in rows of two, all silver too,
Designed with beauty, made with care and love,
By hands shaping with skill, patience and truth,
Cups, each unique with unseen changes, some flaws,
Each cup, perfect, waits hidden from the window light.

Silver Chalice, tarnished and grey, now old and alone,
Stares at the passing crowd, longing,
Looking for the one who will give it a special place,
Alone, now, the cup, can only wait, empty and grey,
Gone is the shining, lost is the pretty and bright,
Missing are the others, all silver, resting in purple and blue,
Just a cup, alone, waiting for morning in the window light.

Reflection

Unknown to you, to me, daily life was writing, within the book of you, everything. Highlighting your daily pain, recording your hidden tears, but leaving easily read hints, in your book, to them.

Notes and Insights

One Day At A Time

Session 9

NOTES OF LIFE LIVED – PULSE AND FLOW

Sometimes, reading the lines of prose transports me to the time when the words were written and flared up in me an unexpected response. Does that mean I am being drawn into the piece and experiencing it as a participant in the pulse and flow of the words? Or, does it mean that I am simply remembering? It is difficult at times to separate the written piece and the response that comes with surrendering to the pulse and flow of the words from the actuality of the day you are currently living.

Often when rereading a piece that was driven from my mind by events, emotions, or in response to an unknown push from within, I am caused to respond. Respond without control or understanding to the piece and become lost in the pulse and flow of the words. Is this a much sought after escape from living life out loud or the taking of the narrow road to the safe place our Creator prepared for us?

Do you really need that question answered? Are you prepared to make the pulse and flow of the words stark, cold, and carry no true weight or no meaning beyond that which is found in a dictionary? If you answer the question, yes, then the pulse and flow of the words is lost to you and in my mind, you are made less.

We are less because the pulse of your life has become stilled, stopped, and you are no longer caught in the flow of life lived out loud. Instead, you see words as only letters joined together with everyday meanings and not as messengers or musicians capable of transporting your heart. Seeing the words and seeking only the technical or literal meaning of each one, and seeing only mundane dictionary meanings, strips the words used in prose of their vitality, of their depth and their ability to create from nothing but the fantasies in our minds. Life has a pulse. Each of us has a life pulse that is only ours.

Others can try to emulate, but the rhythm is always a beat or two off. People can imitate your flow, but the reflection on the passing Life stream is broken by the snatching winds and is not clear. You are made less by living according to someone else's pulse and flow. Diminished by living your life muted, robbing the choir of your voice or the orchestra of your instrument. Living life out loud is not overwhelming others with your rhythm, your pulse, and flow but finding the harmony that lives within you and freeing it. Seeing, hearing, experiencing words of prose as more than just letters combined is part of living life out loud.

Simply Loving
(11 April 2017, Q. Hill)

As my morning prayer ends, my daily sinning begins,
Wrapped in the Joy of a prayer complete, I fall again,
For just beyond Amen, the abyss waits,
And thou, I wear the Armor, in my mind,
There is no escaping the drift of the blowing winds,
As the moments move me away, whisperings begin,
And my joy fades; day becomes bitter to the taste,
That's when the Spirit within seeks and finds,
Sheltering, embracing, simply Loving my Heart.

It's noon, the middle of another difficult day,
Crazy, out of control moments are stealing my praise,
No song of joy, no uplifting, just one burden and another,
Some mine, others delivered, all tearing at the walls,
Walls no longer shielding, no longer strong, just crumbling clay,
And, as the moments escape, on I stumble, blinded and dazed,
My morning's joy faded, the day is a pressure seeking to smother,
That's when the Spirit within seeks and finds,
Sheltering, embracing, simply Loving my Heart.

One Day At A Time

As the day comes to a close, I pray,
Crying from the pain of my sinning, asking for release,
Bowed down, almost broken, at the abyss' edge,
My soul cries out, my heart listens, the silence grows,
And each tear, each moan, melts the day's sins away,
The winds continue to blow, but in my prayer, Peace,
On my knees, bruised and wounded, remembering God's Pledge,
Joy flowered again, fading the day, whispering I Know,
That's when the Spirit within seeks and finds,
Sheltering, embracing, simply Loving my Heart.

Sunday's Mist, Saturday's Dreams
(30 June 2005, Q. Hill)

Sunday's mist washes Saturday's terrors
While we fall endlessly towards yesterday,
Hoping to save ourselves, seeing ourselves
Greatly lifted, validated, without error
Wanting the world, an eagle on a wing,
Lost on accepting, knowing
Tomorrow will be today, then yesterday,
Not promised, not saved,
Then, frightened by the mist of Sunday morn
We cry for Saturday's dreams to be born.

Searching time through shadows media born,
Our salvation we seek, to find Sunday's mist,
But, Saturday's hero we meet.
With sweet lips, cold drinks, forbidden gifts
Tomorrow steals today,
And while we sleep, Yesterday draws near, as,
Sunday's mist covers Saturday's dreams,
Forgiven, the Son rising at last.

One Day At A Time

Speaking of Heroes, Rose
(07 May 2015, Q. Hill)

Speaking of heroes,
Even though, no one asked,
Speaking of you, the one I know,
Who is one today and all days past,

Speaking of heroes,
I recall the pain of a mother lost,
Grip of grief, for years and years, held tight,
I recall the saving Grace, God's first toss,
He sent you, my Loved One, to calm the night, So,

Speaking of heroes,
Not those of fame and flash,
Just Shadows, they come and go,
But, of you, who was my first and my last.

Speaking of heroes,
Even though no one asked,
Speaking of you, the one whom I love,
Given as a gift, the Rose of glorious roses,
You, who accepted God's hardest Task,
Join with a broken vessel, become the morning dove,
God Knew, His Love sent you, you came, love unmasked,

Speaking of heroes,
Willing to carry another's Cross,
Many, just look, point, turn away,
But, you, your love, found me, one of the Lost,
And, whispered, God has the last Say.

Life Spoke

(21 January 2020, Q. Hill)

In the breath of a moment, Life spoke,
Whispering into forever, you,
Calling all to hear, the shouting, the celebration,
When to Day, you first woke.

In startling clarity, the mold broke,
Shapes started drifting, seeking you,
Colors twirled and pirouetted, in elation,
Dreams began to form, ones you invoke.

In the line of Kings and Queen, memories evoke,
Recalling royalty, fresh and new, framing you,
Words, songs and more, await in anticipation,
For the gift in you, of which Life spoke.

In a rush of no need, not losing hope,
The art within seeks release, calling you,
And, the world your canvas, awaits expression,
Don't delay, for in you, Life awoke.

Music Without End

(28 September 2010, Q. Hill)

Broken by the accident of loving you,
Caught, unable to resist, after the smallest taste,
Struggling, minute by minute, with desire,
The storm winds of need, break me again,
Even the rainbow that follows, whispers of you,
And I rush, out of control, to be face to face,
Seeking, needing, cooling for this fire,
Love's solo, playing my heart without end.

Drunken dancing, spinning, grooving, lost,
Your love rhythms, drive me, drum beats roll
Rocking, wave after wave, ocean drenched,
Caught up, moonlight dusted, cool love burning,
Alto sax, gentle solo, winter's first frost,
Chilling, melting, love icy and cold,
Brassy sounds, resting moments, fading inch by inch,
Voices, mellow, calling, with the night's turning,
Love's symphony, playing love notes without end.

One Day At A Time

Blues playing, smoky dreams, endless tears,
Echoes, sweet smells, secret shadows, love and you,
Lonely sounds, water borne, calls yesterday, again,
Brown liquor, empty heart, filled, memories, crying,
Life's river overflows, the rainbow fades, as skies clear,
Melodies pull love hidden deep, breaking me, again,
Broken by the accident of loving you, still hoping,
Love's instrument, playing blues songs without end.

Notes and Insights

One Day At A Time

Session 10

LIVING LIFE, FINDING GRIEF

There are moments when you feel as if there are no more tears left in the world. You have cried them all at least a dozen times. Each of us has these moments, these happenings; if not yet, simply wait. The moment is ahead. The most painful thing for me was when my baby girl, who lives with a very painful condition, was crying, and there was nothing anyone did that seemed to relieve her pain or in the least help her. The doctors would go through their protocols and try this or that, but still she cried, and still I cried with her. Times like this are the most crushing to us. The grief, the pain, we displayed in the overflow of tears is just one type of grief. For many their grief is from the passing of someone close to them, often a family member. The grief caused by the loss of a loved one is somewhat unique in that a person's faith or beliefs can aid you in the acceptance of the beauty of a life lived out loud.

When you brush up against or come face to face with dealing with a life lived out loud now being lived through glimpses of life scenes, there is always a reaction. As well as the often-deep emotional response, I am often overwhelmed with a need to try and capture a glimpse of the life lived.

One Day At A Time

Tear Drops Fall
(7 December 2011, Q. Hill)

Teardrops fall
Each a child too soon called
From a world where sin is truth
Where mothers cry as they let loose
And fathers ask, why so young,
As again the steeple's bell is rung.

Teardrops fall, an ocean they fill
Each a hope, unborn and still
Promises, written, spoken out loud
Lost to fear and growing crowd
No longer shouting, loudly proclaiming,
Anything, but another's shaming.

Tear drops fall, from a cross on high
Forgiveness given with a final cry
Of those also hanging, said one, Lord,
The other, like many, said, if you be god…,
And over our shoulder we look to see
If the world, not Him, sees me.

Living Life, Finding Grief

Tear drops fall, for a life now done
And wondering if you knew the Son
Who called you from the many,
Or were you sold for nickel or a penny
Covered with false praise, unrepented sin
Or blessed, welcomed in?

One Day At A Time

Zion's Song[1]
(13 April 2020, Q. Hill)

Sitting within view, not the last, I see,
Unable to touch, hear your song, sang for me,
Reaching, my heart grasps, sounds of silence,
Coming from a lonely place, on a hill,
Marked by stone, flowers in season, love alight,
As Angels sit, in reverence guard,
Tears, unbidden, again they fall, in daylight, bright,
And, I ask, for the first time, is he alright?

Sweet melodies, my kisses stored, a million or more,
Rhymes, sweet rhythms, Cuddles piled high, in my heart waiting,
Soft lullabies whispered, practiced for you, hummed out loud
Now, forever gazing, looking toward the hill,
Seeing the highest place, Holy, love alight,
Listening for cries, insistent callings, awakening to silence,
And the need to cry, again, gently cradled by the night,
As I ask again, is he alright?

Dreams, life's songs, one after another, gather near,
Mixing, dancing with plans and promises, of things to come,
One of those, two or more of these, love's rhymings,
Holding tight to what will be, the wondrous things I see,
Wishes, possibilities, blessed beyond belief, love alight,
Named for God's City on the Hill, Love's beacon,
Calling, again, the need to hold, your weight so slight,
As I ask again, is he alright?

Tears, a million crystals or more, mine, not for others to see,
Love's melody broken loose, held by the song of him, so sweet,
Hugs, kept, stored, for when again we meet, face to face,
In that City of Light, the Fortress on a Hill,
You, Love Alight, and me, covered by God's Grace,
Marveling, your wings so white, your face, your song so bright,
And, me, needing to cry, again, cradled by Love,
Thanking God, for Zion is alright.

Arise

(31 January 2006, Q. Hill)

Arise, oh wondrous dove,
Spread your love,
Fly, Fly, Arise, oh beautiful one,
Awaken the Day from night's dark rest,
Dance the morning winds
On God's sweet breath,
Causing us, entranced,
For one so truly blessed,
To shed raindrops of joy
As you pass on wings of white,
Fly to Heaven's gate and the Lord's Grace.

Arise, our gift of love,
Spread again your smile, laughter free,
Arise, our joy received,
Kindle the memories of childhood play,
Of giggles and cries, your heart we see,
Growing ever tender, Lord's blessing,
Gentle and sweet,
Fly loving angel,
His gentle arms await,
Hasten with thanksgiving,
Dance the choral strings,
Rising your voice with those singing,
Holy, Holy, Holy

An Ideal, a Hope, and a Promise

Grief takes on many shades of darkness colored only by what loss is being mourned. The darkness looks unrelieved to some who have fallen so deep there is no light to be found. Their everyday life starts with the darkness of unrelenting grief and ends with dreams filled with unquenched tears. Others of us who have fallen into grief find a light or lifeline exists for us to cling to as the darkness seeks to drag us deeper into nothingness of only the pain of what we have lost.

What we have lost that affects us in this way can be any number of things: loss of a favorite pet or object, loss of our home, loss of someone renowned who has affected our lives, loss of a loved one, or the loss of our soulmate. It can also be the loss of a rare opportunity to effect a change of significance, the loss of a statute or icon of historical or personal importance, or the loss of an ideal, a way of life, the hope and promise of the future. In reality, the losses we grieve are personal.

No person can feel the depths of grief you or I may have for something loss simply because they are not you or I. Even with all the knowledge in the world, there are not words to fully and accurately explain your grief. But we must try. Trying often helps with finding the light to led us out of the pit grief can cause us to fall into.

I have spoken of some things that have caused me to grieve. It's personal. I would like to speak a bit about the loss of an icon, an ideal, a hope, and a promise. All of these were lost at the same time, the same moment in history, and those of us who could see, really see, simply cried. Cried for what was lost and wondered why. What am I talking about, the storming of the Capitol, our seat of government and symbol of our ideal, our hope and our promise, by persons, who were the citizens, covered by the Red, White, and Blue flying above the Capitol Rotunda. Lost in the intoxicating power given to those with privilege, they assaulted each of us fighting for those same privileges. Forgotten in their glee of exercising the power of privilege by those covered by the Red, White, and Blue was the damage they were doing and the substantiating of truths spoken about them and the Red, White, and Blue.

I grieve for the loss of lives, so few during the assault, but so many in the wars, fights, and protests to uphold the believed ideal, hope, and promise of living under the Red, White, and Blue. Those covered by the Red, White, and Blue simply exercising their privilege showed by the way they were received and treated that the fight for those not covered was not over and more would be lost. I grieve for those living under the Red, White, and Blue who know the litter being cleaned up after the Capitol assault did not include any of the remnants of weapons used against peaceful protesters. I grieve because many covered by the Red, White, and Blue saw only the assault by those of their privilege taking advantage of their privilege and not the assault on the ideals, hopes and promises of those living under the Red, White, and Blue. In my sadness, I cried. In my grief, I felt the darkness calling. In my heart, I felt strength increasing. In my eyes, I saw why the struggle is necessary. With my promise, I will stand for the hope of we who are currently living under the Red, White, and Blue.

Beginning Of Whatever
(25 July 2008, Q. Hill)

Once you have been to the edge of everything and seen the others standing with you, some lost, some crying from the pain of every day, some just staring, some so broken that they can't stand, some smiling, and some celebrating, you realize the edge of everything is just the beginning of whatever is next.

Once you have been to the foot of the cross and seen the others, some kneeling and begging, some looking upward confused and worried, some just there, some praising and celebrating, and some simply waiting, you know that the foot of the cross is the beginning of whatever is next.

Once you have been to the midnight hour, woken to the pain of broken dreams, lost loves, unresolved issues, wishes never spoken into being, and hear the others waking to the midnight hour, you know that fear is waiting, tears stand ready to fall, pains hidden during the noon hour strain at the bounds, and see that the midnight hour is only the beginning of whatever is next.

Once you have been washed in the blood and seen the other also washed you wonder at the lies told for no reason, the pain given for personal gain, the love withheld without cause, struggle allowed for want of help, the hand uplifted in praise not lower to lift, the tears of joy drying at the church house door, you understand the blood washing is just the beginning of whatever is next.

One Day At A Time

Once you have been to the edge of everything, been to the foot of the cross, been to a midnight hour or two, and have felt the power of the blood washing your sins, you are expected to be ready to step over the edge, accept the gift of the cross, celebrate the coming morning, and share the good news of the sacrifice because you are at the beginning of whatever blessing is next.

Notes and Insights

One Day At A Time

Session 11

SERVICE – LIFE'S SACRIFICE

Speaking of Veterans

(09 November 2018, Q. Hill)

Giving honor where honor is due to those who are now looking back through glass often broken, dirtied and pitted by storm winds that have and continue to crash against it. Speaking of the warriors who stand facing toward forever in defense of home, stand unyielding, facing the rising winds, unturned by assailing debris, unbowed by the pressing weight of the multitude, unturned by the offers of safety, unbroken by the wounds taken.

Recall in awe the stories and tales, spoken by others, seldom by the warriors, some horrific and sad, all true of sacrifice upon sacrifice given by the few chosen to do what most others would not do. Some who still remain so distant, lost, many unknown without a mark or their name. And, of those who returned, some lie among the marching white stones bearing their name, others broken by their service struggle with every day, and of those few, scars hidden, who silently face each day.

One Day At A Time

Giving honor where honor is due is at times given from inside the glass often broken, dirtied and pitted by storm winds by those unmarred by the storms, or by those untouched by the rising dust, or the piercing debris, or the pressing weight of holding the line. But, every time a child asks of, or a mother cries for, or a father recalls moments, and the flag yet waves, another step forth to take their place among the ones who willingly give their all.

With the raising of sun and the setting of day, in rain falling ceaselessly and heat beyond belief, wading through waters filled with danger hidden and known, and in streets filled with hate, or standing resolute before the killing hail and the unending fire, often bending to cover a mother or a child, or kneeling to hand out the gift of life, there will be those to whom honor is due, and they are the same ones who will never ask it of you for the gift they have freely given.

SERVICE – LIFE'S SACRIFICE

We of the First Rank

We, of the first rank, are first seen, first wounded, first to fall, first called and first to stand between now and then.

We, of the first rank, are last to be healed, last to be praised, last to see victory, last to turn from the enemy, last to fall, last to stand between now and then.

We, of the first rank, are not heroes, not great, not small, or significant, not recalled, or even remembered for who we are, we are not alone as we stand between now and then.

We, of the first rank, are weak, transparent, easily harmed, and always dependent on the strength of love, sacrifice, and awe of He that was standing before now and then and when.

One Day At A Time

One More Step
(08 July 2020, Q. Hill)

The warrior sits, alone, staring into the forever past,
Wounds, old and new, call to the always waiting future,
Restless winds blow across memories of battles fought,
Life breezes chill tears for comrades missing and lost,
The warrior recalls promises made, promises kept.

Trumpets play for another, rewarded at the last,
Igniting the need to serve, recalling young, immature,
Among strangers, then as a team, as the art of war was taught,
We each acknowledged the need, accepted it and knew the cost,
When the line was drawn and the call was given, forward we stepped.

In lands foreign and domestic, as warriors, we stand,
Under conditions, any, weather or storm, we face,
Be the rain, water, ice, dust or medal, into it we go,
Through darkness of tunnels or of night driven, light we bring,
Exhausted and hurt, we try to recall when last we slept.

The warrior stands, prepared and scared, reaches out a hand,
To an enemy, a comrade, or refugee, just victims seeking grace,
In landscapes, torn, or neighborhoods like the ones we know
Houses, stores and things, flowers announce the coming spring
With broken hearts, broken dreams it is forward we stepped.

SERVICE – LIFE'S SACRIFICE

Hands, scarred and bent, caress the medals under glass,
Never asked for, never sought, rewards for life's adventures,
Recall for some, heroes all, protests and hate, no parades were given.
Flags held high, salutes raised, the young, our future, march,
The warrior watches, reminded of those lost for whom he wept,
And prays for a peaceful day from days forever past,
Seeing the grave and finally rest in the always waiting future,
Hoping for release for what was done and finally to be forgiven.
As they pass, heads bowed with hearts open, under the rainbow arch,
Warriors prepare for God, Family and Home to take one more step.

Reflections

I am often confronted by the differences of living under the Red, White, and Blue from those who are covered by the Red, White, and Blue. It hurts deeply to know there is one difference, let alone so very many. My children are reaping a harvest they had nothing to do with planting, watering, weeding, or caring for. A harvest made all the more bitter by the washing up of the debris from the centuries' long fight to bring about true and lasting change. My children's children and their children should not have to make again this harvest of being less than those covered by the privileges of being covered by the Red, White, and Blue. Nor should they have to walk through the debris of lies told to those who fight for truth and lasting change.

Notes and Insights

One Day At A Time

Session 12

SPEAKING OF LIFE – LIVED

Telling life stories, through words that speak with emotions and power of life lived in all the colors of the rainbow, is a joy. Stories not only of the bright and beautiful colors often seen arching across the sky after a rainstorm, or the ones drawn to illustrate the primary colors of red, blue, green and yellow, but also of the other colors, some dark and frightening. The stories called from these dark colors often reflect the vivid purples, dark blues and deep reds that highlight the wounds, some hidden beneath layers of scars and smiles to deflect the eyes. These life stories are of the pains, the protests, and the loss, they're of the heroes that often appear to pick through the debris and find something worth fighting for, saving, loving, or finding simple beauty in the darkest of moments.

I would like to share a story with you, a walk through a time in a young man's life. The story begins happily enough. He and his girlfriend were having dinner at her home. The love each had for the other was clearly evident, but there was a tension. The young man did not know one of life's train wrecks waited just before the happy ending. Dinner ended with laughter and drinks, a bit of television, and then his girl suggested they go to bed early. There followed what seemed to be hours of talk, play, and lovemaking. In the early, early morning hour, the girlfriend asked the young man to talk. Unaware of what was coming, the young man smiled, stroked her face, then noticed her crying. Concerned, he asked, "What's wrong?

His girlfriend looked at him through her tears and said, "This is our last time together. My boyfriend will be home from prison tomorrow." Caught completely by surprise, they were going on two years together; they made plans and all that, he asked if she was sure. She said, "Yes." The young man began to cry because he could see how broken her own words made her and because he loved her so much. As he began to ask why and become upset, his girlfriend asked him to leave. Just like that he knew there were no more words, no more pleas, and no more bright colors of love. So, he dressed, crying, unable to look at the pain of her tears.

Dressed, he stepped out into the freezing Detroit winter. The temperature, easily below zero degrees, and it had snowed during the night. Extremely poor, the young man's clothing did little to keep the freezing cold from being painful. Hurting so badly from the news just received, he hardly noticed it. As he walked through the frozen streets, dark houses on all sides, he wondered how to go on. Why to go on. Through the tears that still flowed, freezing on his face, he noticed car lights on the otherwise deserted streets. Knowing no one stopped in the ghetto to pick anyone up, he was surprised as the car slowed. The car stopped next to him and suddenly there was a spotlight on him. In Detroit, during those years, a group of police called the "Big Four" terrorized the neighborhoods. The Big Four were four cops, one uniformed cop usually driving, and three plain clothed cops riding along. The Big Four made it their business to hassle, beat, arrest, and kill young blacks, especially the young men. Their reputation was so dire that given the opportunity, you ran and ran hard because either you got away, or you got whatever was on their minds to do. And the car with the spotlight belonged to the Big Four.

No one around, anyway who interfered with the Big Four? Doing that only added you to the ones getting abused, arrested, and maybe shot. Complaining fell on deaf ears and resulted in an increase in Big Four patrols. So if you had the chance, you ran. The young man was caught, not only by the spotlight, but also by the shotgun pointed at him out the back window of the car. So, he stopped and faced the car knowing normally these encounters did not end well. A voice from the car said, "What are you doing out here?" The young man answered, "Leaving my friend's house and going home." The voice asked, "Do you have any weapons or drugs?" "No", answered the young man. The voice then demanded, "Take off your coat." No sense arguing with the shotgun, so the young man took off his coat and dropped it on the ground. The voice said, "I can't see if you have a weapon hidden under your sweater. Take off your sweater and shirt." When the young man hesitated, the voice demanded again as another window of the car came down and another gun was pushed out toward him. The young man, shivering from the intense cold, complied by taking off his sweaters and shirts and dropped them to the snow-covered sidewalk. Hoping it was enough, the young man turned around to show he had no hidden weapons. How very mistaken, his abuse had just started.

The voice demanded, "Take off your pants." The young man protested, and the voice asked calmly, "You want to get shot and left to die?" "No sir", replied the young man as he began to unbuckle his belt and lower his pants. The voice demanded, "I said take them off, nigga!" Left without a choice, the young man removed his tennis shoes and pulled his pants off. Standing there unable to stop shaking, the heartbreak from the words his girlfriend said earlier forgotten, and the tears freezing on his face, the young man prayed for it to be over. The voice accompanied by laughter from within the car, demanded, "Take off your drawers, boy." The young man, crying even harder, because he knew what was next was going to be really bad, refused. The voice said, quietly, "Take off your drawers. Do it now." Again, the young man refused. The rear car door opened and a big white cop got out with the shotgun in his hand. He pushed the young man down and said, "Pick up those rags and get in the car." The young man complied and a big cop pushed him into the back seat where another cop was waiting.

Overwhelmed by the sudden heat of the car the young man gasped, still afraid, his tears, thawing, flowed down his cheeks. The cop got in, placing the shotgun upright between his legs and slamming his elbow into the young man's chest, knocking the wind from his lungs. Then the other cop began punching and elbowing the young man. Whatever words they were saying were lost in the pain of the blows.

The driver of the police car drove to the warehouse area near the river and stopped. The cop, who was in the car when the young man got in, opened his door and grabbed the young man, pulled him out. After hitting and kicking him, he started to pull his weapon, just then the police radio went off. The uniformed cop answered it and called to the cop standing over the young man, saying, "We got to go." With a final kick, the cop got into the car and the police car drove off. Dressing, the heart-broken and beaten young man, looked at the beginning morning light without hope. Further from home, freezing and hurting badly, and fearing the Big Four may come back, he started walking because he knew there would be no kind words, no pleas, and no bright colors of love.

Sunday's Mist

(11 May 2005, Q. Hill)

Sunday mist washes Saturday's Terrors,
While we fall endlessly toward yesterday,
Hoping to see ourselves greatly lifted, validated,
Wanting the world, lost on accepting,
Knowing, tomorrow will be today, then yesterday
But, frighten by the mist of Sunday morning,
Crying for Saturday's dreams,
We wish for the day's end and tomorrow.

In the shadows of the moment of your regrets,
There is no solace, no enduring endearment,
Just the flickering of things dreamed,
Things thought and released,
Released as Saturday's dreams,
To be caught by someone other than you,
You hope the dreams never end or tomorrow begin.

One Day At A Time

In the darkness of unfilled moments,
As Sunday mist washes Saturday's Terror,
Your yesterday regrets assault today's hopes,
No shining or glowing light of accomplishment.
Just the permanent ink of things written,
Imprinted on the cloth of your life,
Being read today by someone other than you,
As we wish for tomorrow and today's end

Speaking of Life – Lived

The joyous notes of life's rhythm set the tempo to living. Often these notes are stolen, creating a void. Silenced, vacant, and exposed we seek peace at the end of the day to restart the song.

Words, with all life's nuances can be a comfort with the ability to bridge the pain from daily living. Even when telling of the everyday struggles, words are colored by the emotions and power of life lived in all the colors of the rainbow.

Without a question, of forgiveness
(7 December 2011, Q. Hill)

Let's speak, for real, for real, today,
About everyday crying, as Jesus wept,
While preachers preach, and churches fill,
Of causal beatings of a priest, in a church,
Of Kids taken, abused and thrown, away,
Like trash on Dead Man's Hill,
As Lies told, not guilty, they plead,
Without a question, of forgiveness, Stop it, please.

Caught by the evening news, life's drama on display,
Of the everyday happenings, as the faithful slept,
Mothers crying, as their babies lie still,
Lives taken, for a slight or hurt,
Fathers, missing, no protector are they,
Denying, their part, refusing the bitter pill,
As Lies told, not guilty, they plead,
Without a question, of forgiveness,
Stop it, please.

Speaking of Life – Lived

Dressed in fancy clothes, like costumes on Halloween Day,
Just wrappings, for promises, spoken, not kept,
As sin, like the flu spreads, and only joy it kills,
While shouting and holy dancing, tramples hope in the dirt.
Behind church house walls, where the holy stay,
Praying for salvation, as another child lies still,
As Lies told, not guilty, they plead,
Without a question of forgiveness,
Stop it, please.

One Day At A Time

Black, Brown, You
(02 June 2020, Q. Hill)

Hear, again, the sounds of yesterday's crying,
Loudly proclaiming today's shame,
The sobs of children born, torn and alone,
Watching the whips fall again in a place called home,
Mothers and fathers, crying for a son,
Hear again, those seen as less loudly proclaimed,
By voices colored by anything but black, brown, you.

On street corners, in alleys and on highways,
Lost, like addicted whores, and homeless veterans,
Unseen by ones passing in search of the promised dream,
Left to wonder at the doors so tightly closed
The ceilings forever lowered glass no more.
Screaming for attention, asking for restitution,
Promised, Forty acres and a mule, by liars and the law,
With scars still showing, bleeding fresh and new,
Stands silhouettes of people colored black, brown, you.

Speaking of Life – Lived

Hands lifted, cries loud, neither of praise,
Are of no use or consequence, as bullets blaze,
Pleads of need often simply to breathe,
Ignored, as the pressure tightens, killing the praise,
Another lies dead or dying, surrounded by police blue,
Cries, loud and demanding, why?
Why did he have to die, another mother, pleads
Surrounded by blue, reasons why, spoken,
Lies, hiding the bitter truth, of yesterday's crying,
Hear again, strange fruit, proclaiming today's shame,
Swaying in an unchanged wind, as again, the whip falls,
Striking, scarring anew, people colored black, brown, you.

ONE DAY AT A TIME

Mother Sits
(9 May 2011, Q. Hill)

Married or not, under the broken church steeple,
Looking through the window of yesterday,
There are pictures, faded and clear,
With movie trailers of days, nights, things and people,
Life past, future foretold, shown on video display
Framed moments, silent stills, imagined stories to hear
Mother sits staring, quietly smiling.

In the Words, spoken or not, life unfolds,
There would be great grief, pain and hate,
The world would spin not around, but down
With Life, Love and Fear out of control
Children raised, decisions made, bitter is the taste,
Of wearing the unsought, unreturnable crown,
Mother sits staring, quietly recalling.

So much time spent, waiting,
Paused between what was and what is
Keeping it moving, between now and when,
Day by day, life's print, dark lines tracing,
A Queen, not Elizabeth, simply Liz,
Her throne of grace, gifted by a Friend,
Mother sits, quietly crying.

Speaking of Life – Lived

No yesterday's apologies, spoken,
No pictures too dark, too bright, to hide,
No dress, old or new, covering wounds
Just another morning, to greet, wide open,
More images, collected, then sat aside,
Closet full, waiting dreams, sweet blues tunes
Mother sits, quietly humming.

One Day At A Time

Broken Panes
(14 June 2020, Q. Hill)

Looking through broken panes,
At memories rushing by, flashes,
Sometimes bright and gay, laughter,
Of days young, free, love-filled and me,
Dancing the neighborhood streets,
Streets tree-lined, clean and home,
Mother, calling us to dinner, from our play,
Father waiting, work hardened, smiles, too.
But, now, grandmother, you stare,
Through broken pains at our yesterday home, now gone.

Looking through broken panes,
At people rushing by, no one pauses,
Sometimes they look, seeing rotten plaster,
Signs of days, old, ruined, fear-filled and me,
Pavement, cracked, dirty and no longer home,
Mother, now passed away, cried for yesterday,
Father, gone too, first broken, by promises, too,
Grandmother, you, with rent due, stares,
Through broken pains at the ghetto, now home.

Speaking of Life – Lived

Looking through broken panes,
At headstones standing, today and those past,
Sometimes the graves call, speaking names,
Heroes, past, of young lost to life and blue, me,
Mother, beaten and jailed, marched for today,
Father, cried for sons and daughters, lives stolen, too,
And, Grandmother, you, stand hands upraised, stares,
Through broken pains, tear gassed, seeing troops, not home.

Looking through broken panes,
At memories rushing by, flashes,
Sometimes, no, often dark and troubled, sadness,
Of today no longer young, or love-filled and me,
Walking the neighborhood, no, the ghetto streets,
Streets, crime and homeless-lined, no longer called, home,
Mother, watched, governments take away our play,
Father, work hardened, recalled, his stolen votes, too.
Grandmother, you, hear again yesterdays' promises, stares,
Through broken pains, smiles stealing again today's home.

One Day At A Time

Walking Through Our Gardens

The young man, a child really, got off the bus after a four-day bus ride from his Mama's house to be met by his uncle. This was expected as Big Mama did not have a car or even drive. What happened next was not expected. It was near the beginning of the school year, and it was to be the child's first year. His uncle did not drive to Big Mama's house but took the main highway instead. The child had learned not to ask questions of adults that may be unwelcomed. He sat and watched the landscape roll pass, not asking questions and even though he wanted to know why they were not going to Big Mama's house, he remained quiet. When they arrived, it was at his uncle's home, miles and miles from Big Mama. His uncle opened the car door and told him to get out. Gripping the small suitcase with his clothes and the shoebox which had contained the lunch Mama had made him four days before, the child complied.

They entered the house and were met by his aunt, the uncle's wife. The young man was left standing in the hallway as they greeted each other and discussed the ride home. His aunt called to him, saying "come in the kitchen" and asked if he was hungry. While he ate what was provided, his aunt was preparing a bowl of something. Once she was finished, she spoke to his uncle. His uncle turned to him and told him to come with them. They walked down the hall to a room; his uncle told him this is your room.

I know this beginning is strange and leaves a lot to be questioned, so let me help. The young man was silent because his asking questions was simply not accepted and could result in a hitting or beating. He was on the bus because Mama had for whatever reason run out of time or need for him to be around. When that happened, he and his brothers were always sent away, usually to Big Mama's house. Mama was an abused woman living in a time when people just looked away. Without family near, she was always available to be victimized. The children were at times added fun for the young man's stepfather. It may have been that sending them away was Mama's way of protecting them. We don't know because she never said that. The young man and his brothers spent a lot of time with Big Mama and some time with an aunt or uncle. So what was happening was not that strange to the child, but what happened next was.

Everyone recalls an incident from their past that remains as fresh as a just poured cup of morning coffee. Those incidents are like the coffee having a strong aroma and the heat of it can burn you if you are not careful. It doesn't matter what the incident was or when it occurred, what matters is the impression it had on you. Maybe the impression it is still having on you. I looked into that flawed reflection and not one incident, but many, leaped for recognition. The incidents want to be included in this narrative, each recalling the happenings in their own unique way, and each true one way or the other.

Childhood happenings that have stayed fresh through adulthood are like tattoos, well intentioned, unique, and message-driven, indelible, and now somewhat indistinct. At least when a child, as an adult or when older, thinks of the incident, it gives those involved some ownership. And having some ownership is important to the beginning of finding your way to a safe place, maybe even some healing. The tears, held or secretly released, which at the time they were initially released appeared to be wasted, left an impression on the soul of the child. Those tears will be cried again silently or out loud whenever life once again causes the adult to recall the child. Some of those tears are cried so often they become personal friends who visit whenever they want and must be greeted, or they will tear down whatever you have built in your life. The incident with the child caused tears silent and heavy to remain though adulthood and even now as we recall. Tears cried as a wounded and helpless child color every day lived as the memories seek to become the reality of the day you are currently living.

The room the uncle showed the child was huge to the young man. It had a bed, a closet, a place by the window with a heating grate to play. It also had what appeared to be a large baby crib. The crib was occupied by a person; a very skinny and twisted person. His aunt walked over to the crib and touched the person, speaking softly. The person made sounds, not words just sounds. The child was immediately frightened and wanted to run. The child wanted to get out of the room as quickly as possible. But that was not to be, his uncle turned, grabbing lightly his shoulder, pushed, pulled him to the edge of the crib, forcing him to look at the person in the crib. What he saw was a twisted individual, mostly naked except for a big cloth wrapped around his middle. How did the child know the person was a man? The person did not have any breasts or such. The child's uncle spoke, saying "you are here to keep (the person's name was lost in the fearful screaming noise in the child's head) company until we arrange for his care." "This is your room. You can go to the bathroom, the kitchen, but nowhere else in the house unless we tell you it is alright. You can eat only what we sat out for you and please, do not mess up this room." The child had no response. His aunt was also talking, but the child could not hear or understand her. She left the room and came back with a big bag of metal toy soldiers. Speaking to the child's uncle, she handed it to him, and he presented it to the child.

You, the reader, have to understand, the child was not used to receiving gifts, especially toys. So he did not at first reach out to take the soldiers. He just stood there lost as to what was happening or what to do. Wasn't he supposed to be starting school soon? The child even then loved reading and learning, and he was excited about going to school. Maybe the toy soldiers were being given to fill the void caused by not going to school. The child was never told.

His uncle pushed the toy soldiers into the child's hand saying these are yours to play with. He also began to explain why the child was there instead of at Big Mama's house. He was to stay with the person during the day when his uncle and aunt were away from the house. This was his job. He didn't have to change the cloth, feed, or even talk to the person. He was to call the numbers by the phone if the person was making loud noises or seemed to stop breathing. Nothing else, that's how the child was to spend what was to be their first year of school. After a while, the child could ignore the person in the crib as he played with the toy soldiers and imagined great battles and such. The toy soldiers, his first gift that was his alone, became the center of his world. He played with them and at night he slept with one in his hand. Then one day his uncle came in and told the child to pack his things, he was going to Big Mama's house. The child was overjoyed; actually, crying real tears so great was his joy.

Before they left for Big Mama's house, some men came with a rolling bed to take the person away. His aunt stood crying as she watched them taking the person away. Shortly after they left, his uncle said it was time to go. The child grabbed his small suitcase and the bag of precious toy soldiers, his friends. The bag wasn't complete because one of the toy soldiers had fallen through the heating grate and the child could not reach it. As the child walked to the door, his aunt reached out and took the bag of toy soldiers. No words were spoken; she just took them back and held them to her chest as she continued to cry. The child wanted to say something, ask for them back, but knew better. He swallowed more tears and followed his uncle to the car. He looked at the window above the heating grate and said goodbye to the lost toy soldier, crying within for the toy soldier who was now alone, like him.

Lasting impressions of significant incidents are like statues in our mind's garden sharing the space with wandering memories and life pictures grayed by the passage of time. The Garden has sounds drifting on the sometimes-gentle breezes but also shouting when life actions trigger violent storms to rage within the garden. The statutes endure the storms and life raging as well as the destruction caused by winds blowing fiercely through. The statutes, significant incidents, made solid by their impact, known and unknown, on the mind and the garden within. The Garden also has flowers, incidents, recalling the times when life lived out loud brought you such joy. The statutes remain to recall for us the life incidents that caused them to be drawn from the canvas of our lives and made permanent in our minds' Garden. Have you visited your Garden, walked among the statutes recalling the incidents captured in them?

Speaking of Life – Lived

Why Can't You...
(05 April 2021, Q. Hill)

Why can't you love me as I want to be loved?
Why can't you feel the pain within me longing for you?
Why can't you see the wounds over the scars?
Why can't you feel the pain of love sought, day by day?
Why can't you reach out your heart and catch mine?
Why am I so alone when standing with you?

Questions that assault my restless sleep,
Calling me to wake and dream, long for you,
Forcing the night to flee, hide before your light,
Causing me to gasp, out of breath, broken, crying out,
Seeking, trying to hold the dream, but, like fading smoke,
It leaves the aroma, the remembrance of love from you.

Words, so many words are spoken,
Each stripped of what is said and what is meant,
And, phrases, like dried leaves, crushed by your step,
Try to recreate truth, find the truth of what is lost,
But, the breeze of love left too long alone, blows,
Lifting and scattering the broken pieces of love once so true.

One Day At A Time

So, why can't you love me as I want to be loved?
So, why can't you feel the pain of me longing for you?
So, why can't you see the wounds over now scars?
So, why can't you feel my pain and love seeking you, day by day?
So, why doesn't your heart simply reach out and catch mine?
So, why can't I say I'm alone when standing with you?

Just Another Lonely Day
(10 June 2005, Q. Hill)

Just another lonely day, looking for my blessing
For the Savior to come my way

Is the Word of God just window dressing?
Just promises thrown my way,
Is Jesus really my Lord?

I'm lost, listening for words,
For your presence, today
Please, just touch me,
Jesus, Jesus, Please?

Just another lonely day, looking for a blessing
For my Savior to come my way

Lost, listening for you in the distance
Jesus, my Jesus, find me please

Just another lonely night, hiding my tears, my shame,
Is my faith enough, will my Savior come, call my name?

One Day At A Time

Standing broken, unshaken, praising, worshiping, crying
Jesus, Jesus, my True Lord

Lost in your presence, your glory, touch me, just touch me,
Lord Jesus, Please

Just another lonely day, looking for a blessing
For my Savior to come my way

Notes and Insights

One Day At A Time

Session 13

LOVE, LIVED OUT LOUD

Each day, we are given an opportunity to love again: to replay love already lived, to speak of love to someone lost and blue, to touch someone with the gentleness of love shared, and to recall the world without love is empty and cold. Love shelters and protects us while exposing our hearts to pain unbelievable, and while filling to overflowing, love lost leaves us empty and aching in ways that simply cannot be explained, only experienced. I have heard of people shunting love, hiding from it, often in plain sight. Why? There are a million reasons given, all valid, but for me the one that makes no sense is that love is a waste of time. Is breathing a waste of time? We were made to love and love greatly. Yes, love has occasion to hurt and hurt deeply, but you cannot feel the joy of love shared without the risk of love gone. And, trust me there is no greater joy than love shared.

Like the multicolored crystal light from a diamond held under the light of the morning sun, love shines on each of us. What beauty is shown when we allow love to shine through. Also, like the multihued light, love has many colors, each with its own distinct essence. Any description given will lack something and fall short of the love felt and shared by someone else. It would be easier to capture the wind in a bag full of holes than to capture all the facets of love. Even though we know these things to be true, we are each called to describe the joy that explodes our heart and leaves us breathlessly wanting to experience it again. This love lived out loud.

DO YOU LOVE ME, THEN?
(04 April 2006, Q. Hill)

When the landscape of life is earthquake shaken,
Will you stand with me?
When the flood tide rises drowning our dreams,
Will you tread with me?
When the dogs of despair howl night after night,
Will they shout back with me?
When fire has burned and only ashes remain,
Will you replant with me?
When tower sags under the weight of the years,
Will you rise with me?
When the foundations shake, tremble and break,
Will you rebuild with me?
All this is just to ask will you be there,
When my face is wrinkled,
My pants are wet, smelly too,
My snores are loud, wet too,
My desire is gone, ability too,
My drive is low, juices too,
My winds blows, excuse me, too,
When God has called me, and I have left you,
Do you love me, then?

Impromptu and You
(17 August 1987, Q. Hill)

A message for,
Written in nothing, unseen,
Saying things, quietly,
Inside yourself,
And leaving footprints on your mind,
But, changing nothing, everything,
These words are written in nothing.

Something about thoughts,
Beginning in you, seeking,
Speaking to no one, loudly,
Yet touching the endings, dreams,
You've hidden away
And finding secrets,
Not yours to freely give,
Just thoughts about something,
Something waiting, too long within.

Love, Lived Out Loud

Smiling, my heart knowing,
It's too late for darkness, closing,
Too early, much, for me to speak,
But my heart knowing,
Gives nothing away,
Yet tells on me, again,
And leaves me breathless,
Hiding from the loneliness,
I would let the darkness in,
But my heart smiling, knowing,
Betrays me to love, impromptu
And you again.

One Day At A Time

Confessions of Heart Broken
(01 September 2011, Q. Hill)

Crystal notes from a glass empty,
Sound loudly in Love's last space
Accompanied by the blues man's guitar,
A melody, deep and complete, sung alone,
Whispered words, the Broken Heart singing.

Wanted to fall in love, and love simply
But why, bitter after the sweetest taste,
Love hurts, leaving unhealed scars,
While feeling so good, even when gone,
Heart Broken, our last Kiss dreaming.

Love's ache, down Deep, fills me,
Pushing Joy and Happiness out of place,
Darkness, draws, complete, night without stars,
Like Love's answer, the busy tone,
Broken cries, Heart's tears streaming.

Play another sad song, please,
One that slows Heart's mad race,
And stops the Tears, about to start,
As again, memories, Love alive,
Break the restrains, so careful placed,
Heart again sings, sad Melodies moan.

Days of wondrous play
(04 April 2006, Q. Hill)

Days of wondrous play,
Your happiness pushing sadness away,
And the joy of things simple,
Teased smiles to sadden eyes,
As your friendship, unending,
Is shown in your patience stance.

Try once, try twice, until it's right,
Now, over again, success and treat,
Joy between friends, something to eat.
Wait, not fast, there's more, make it last,
No, begging won't help you,
Snuggling will not do,
Oh, stop your flirt!
You're teasing me again.

One Day At A Time

Tear-stained memories wait,
Sheltering a friendship without end,
Sad moments seek my joy,
Then, recalling your smile,
Your laugher and play,
The expectant wait, soft whine,
Forget the treat, the favorite toy,
Remember instead,
The soft rubbing of your head,
Warm loving of a forever friend,
Sharing each other every day.
Recalling this, please smile.

Love Is...

Love is an easy thing when all you have to do is provide, hug, guide, and simply worry about what the future will bring. It changes completely when there are no flowers, smiles, cuddly or soft things, and the end just is not in sight. How to deal with it? I firmly believe you are not given more than you can handle. That does not mean what you are given is going to be just extremely difficult. It means that what you are given may be impossible. Know that it may be impossible for anyone, but you. I have heard stories of mothers doing unbelievable things to save their children, things like lifting cars or moving immense objects. We all marvel at these events and discount them as one of those good things.

There are stories of unreal sacrifice by parents to make a way for their children to succeed or make it another day. Things like a parent throwing themselves in the path of an object barreling down on their child to save them. We wonder if we could do that and hope we never have to find out. When your child is going through, no matter how many times, or how long, you will find what is needed to keep doing the things they need. This is the impossible thing that outsiders really don't understand: where does the strength come from? The other side of love is not hate as so many think, at least not for some of us. It is more love, and every time you turn it, there is more love. That love is where the strength comes from; it swells up, blossoming new whenever it is needed.

I know that sounds all high-browed, full of it, but what about when you get tired, when you just run out of energy? It seems that your batteries have been completely drained and still the life crisis goes on. Where is the energy, the love, then? Wait, for those of you that have gone through, stop, and don't say it. Those that have not gone through, they just don't know. Let me try to say it.

One way to look at love is to picture walking up a hill, and no matter how close to the top you get, you never reach it. Add to that weather, you know the nasty rainy, cold miserable kind of weather that makes going forward just hard. Add fog that surrounds you blocking out the sun with sounds that are all kind of weird and the ground under your feet is slippery with mud and stuff. You know the kind of situation where you want to just stop and give up, but you can't because the walk you are making is for someone you love more than life itself and to stop is just unthinkable. It has nothing to do with your physical or mental strength; those may fail you, but love is more, and true love has all the strength you need. Love is strong; it is also not easy.

There are moments when you feel as if there are no more tears left in the world. You have cried them all, at least a dozen times. The most painful thing for me is when my baby is crying, and there is nothing that seems to help her. The doctors go through their protocols trying this or that procedure, but still she hurts and cries, and still I cry with her. Times like this are the most crushing to us: our loved one is in need, and all we can do is not what is needed. We are fully engaged with our child, the doctors, nurses, and techs, but nothing any of us are doing appears to help. Oh, that's not to say they are not doing all they can but to say it is simply not enough. And, my child, my loved one, still cries.

Days when my daughter's pain is out of control are few when measured against a year. But when seen only through the window of time while the pain is occurring, the hours, minutes, and seconds each are eons, forever long! You are told it will take only ten minutes for the meds to work and to give them a chance. Imagine watching someone burn and telling them, the fire engine is on the way. Do you think they really care about it being on the way? The only thing to them is what they are going through right then, and how very painful it is. But, wait, we were talking about the parents and the impact this has on their love.

For me, sometimes it is like walking barefoot on extremely hot pavement. This is something I know a lot about from my childhood in Las Vegas. Hot was real hot and we kids were not always smart. Well, anyway, at first when you step on the pavement it is painfully obvious you should not do this but still you decide you can take it and go on. But the further you get out onto the concrete, the hotter it gets, until you simply can't take it anymore and decide to get back to shade. It is then you realize how very far you have come and that there is no relief anywhere near. Going back is not an option, so you press forward hoping it will be over soon. Knowing that when you get off the hot pavement, you are going to have to deal with your very painfully burned and hurt feet. So, it is with watching your child go through except there is no going back for you or them.

How to deal with it? To begin with, know that you are not just a spectator but an active participant whose role is absolutely key to the situation. You can either be a relief or a burden; it is all in what you do and how you do it. Me, I upset my baby. Yes, that's right; I get her to focus her attention and anger at having to go through the pain on me. She gets upset and will typically say to me, "Dad, just go and leave me alone. Where's Mom?" I will say, "What you don't want me here? Well, I'm not going anywhere, so stop whining." About then she is being beat up pretty badly by the pain and will say quietly, "Dad, I know what you are doing, but it's not working right now. So, please stop." Right then, I cry, but not where she can see. I hide my tears and engage her in a conversation about anything for as long as she can focus on it. That's the first thing you must know, you help in any way you can. Do not stop being the parent, the protector, the love that surrounds. This is the time when all the love you profess will be tested beyond your ability to understand.

Childhood Joys I See

(12 November 2006, Q. Hill)

Off in the distance, motion I see,
Sounds of singing and laughter come to me,
Jumping and running, tumbling free
Children at play
In the age-old way,
I feel the tug,
The pull of desire,
But I know I would quickly tire,
So I smile and even laugh
At the childhood joys I see.

Reflections

Love is hard, demanding and all that. Love is all the tenderness in the world covered by joy so complete it consumes you. I am surprised at the amount of love that remains after living life out loud and surviving to this point.

Love, Lived Out Loud

Sessions in Love, In Love with You

Caught in the everyday struggle of just living, we often find ourselves brushed, caressed by unexpected and intense feelings. These feelings break free from the bindings of mind and free of the living we do day by day. There is often longing for the sight of, or the hearing of, or touch of someone who has broken into your private places and ravaged one of your most closely guarded sanctuaries, your heart. And now you are caught wanting more. Wanting to completely immerse yourself in the shark-filled ocean of their love and simply be loved in return. How do you express the intensity of release when your love overcomes you causing your body, your heart, your life essence to lose itself completely giving your everything to another? What words or phrases are sufficient? Can you even begin to explain or to compare the completeness you experience when your love is caressed, held and allowed to go beyond the edges of reality into the presence of glory colored by your passions released without bounds?

Yes, we are talking about love between two people and about love of one for another regardless of whether the love is felt by both. Love like that does not ask permission, care about your plans, or even think of being polite; it only cares about being expressed and expressed one to one. Love is a gift directly from God, tailor-made for each of us. Love is designed by God to cover you with His Grace and Mercy.

Again, the question is how to explain the completeness true love gives you. For me, the answer is simple: trust God, who is Love, and give in to the experiences only true love can provide. One warning: love is truly a two-sided beast with one side being love without measure and the other side colored by every emotion opposite of love and often hurting, hurting more than anything you have ever experienced. Know also the love within you does not care about the darkness of the other side. Love only wants your body, your heart, your life essence to lose itself completely in sharing God's gift with another.

(untitled)

(10 June 2010, Q. Hill)

As the Dust of sweet surrender, yours, settles,
My Breath sighs as the heat, outward, flows,
No longer Covered, me, dirty or wet,
I relax in the Gift, received, for an apology given,
And, the Moment, ours, begins Again,
As Sweet Surrender, blossoms, and Joy awaits!

One Day At A Time

In Love with You

When talking about being in love with another person, I am often left trying to recall when I first fell in love. It needs to be understood that my interaction with ladies has always been colored by my relationship with Mama. She was an abused woman whose children, including me, were everyday witnesses with no power to intervene. Love for me was Big Mama and my brothers, and later, my sister. The feelings for everyone, especially ladies, were something else. Even today I cannot provide an accurate description of the feeling. I just know it was not love. Being an avid reader, I have read a lot about love, all the different shapes and types of love. I have watched hundreds of movies with various love-based themes. As a result, I have often wondered, "Why not me?"

It is not just that the scenes played out in books and on the big screen are not played out in my life, but also, the obvious feelings one for the other on display. Yes, I got caught in that sex is a love trap and found it to be true; love is not sex and sex is not love. Of course, real love making can be an expression of true love. There is completeness in giving yourself totally to another person and receiving all of them in return. I know this, but my reality has often not included my giving totally of myself or trusting that my love partner is giving totally of themselves. This doubt makes finding and returning true love extremely hard. Love of me for a long, long time was a room with many exit doors, and I was always near one of them.

That is not to say my heart was shielded from the lure and traps of love. It was not. In fact, just the opposite was often true. You see, I created in my mind the image of what the love of my life would be for me. She would be all that, extremely beautiful, smart, graceful and totally dedicated to me. She would have an unbelievable smile with a gorgeous personality and faith in our Lord God. She would change the atmosphere in every room she entered and all would be impressed with her just being herself. In my mind finding her would be simply because she would find me. And, she did.

To say I was shocked when the love of my life approached me is a gross understatement. Yes, she did it through a friend because I had failed to approach her. I had seen her a number of times before and even had spoken with her at least once. How could I not have noticed she was beautiful, articulate, smart and very special in every way? But I was caught up in my own world and working very hard at just making it, so making the connection that she was the gift I had always sought just did not happen. But she knew and acted on that knowledge by taking the first real steps. The night we truly met, we talked and talked. It seemed I was the echo to her voice, my heart simply soared. I believe I was overcome by her from the first we spoke that evening and I am still overcome by her all these years later.

We began dating, seeing each other quite often becoming more and more involved. All was well, or appeared to be. Remember those demons I mentioned before. They did not go away or even take a break. Instead, those demons pressed ever harder, reminding me of my unworthiness, of my pain and loss, of my inability to love past the sex. The demons reminded me love of the type I was feeling and receiving just was not for me. So, I left.

One Day At A Time

The Morning Calls
(28 October 2011, Q. Hill)

The morning calls you,
And, you answer with the joy of being loved,
As the day beckons, over your shoulder you see passion,
Torn, love again, or let the day begin?

With the freshness of loves last kiss
You move, the rhythms of passion drive you,
To rise again in joy, as the morning calls,
And the day beckons, insisting on attention,
You find ecstasy's climatic release,
Falling gently, interrupted by ringing alarm bell.

As again, you rise to the joy of having loved,
The day frowns at time wasted, lost in passion,
And with hesitant haste, you wash the evidence away,
Now, smiling, you close the door on love's last kiss,
Answering the day's calling you,
Tasting, savoring the joy of having been loved.

So, What Does This Say
(27 June 2006, Q. Hill)

Frosted window glass hides the crystal views,
Obscuring the whispered comments of the lips we read,
Causing our despair to rise screaming to the future,
And the joys so deeply guarded to dissipate with the winds,
So, what does this say of our love, discussed?

Chilled juices, a paper, shadows of today's news,
Opinions, events, shared to fit our perceived need,
And supposing we are all cosmopolitan, mature,
Glad smiles, close not-friends, props needed to blend in,
So, what does this say of our love, those trusted?

Windshield wipers like secret lies wipe away the clues,
Ice-bound, crushed by the pressure our hearts plead,
Penciled notes, passed hand-to-hand, childish, unsure,
Tear-stained cheeks rose-pedaled scents, happening again,
So, what does this say of our love, joy-filled balloons, busted?

Sunburned fog flees exposing hidden valleys, truths,
Words spill falling helplessly planting unwanted seed,
With increasing weight, dreams sag covered by life's manure,
High-walled maze, lost, but, the scent, of love and friend,
So, what does this say of our love, real or one, lusted?

One Day At A Time

Multicolored light world out of focus, just you,
Breathless beauty, saffron and pink my heart freed,
Gone, yesterday, lost, tomorrow, only today, so sure,
Whispered comments, shocking your beauty, now it begins,
So, what does this say of our love?
Blessed, diamond dusted, a starlit fantasy,

Night Rose, Passion Rose (con't)
(09 April 1986, Q. Hill)

In the chilling breeze, imagined,
Creeping through the closed,
Yet open, greenhouse door,
Night Rose,
Passion Rose withers,
Drooping as never before,
Thorns exposed, attacking,
Not protecting anymore
And slowly a petal falls,
As the fantasy is made to wait.

In the quiet interlude, as the day ends,
Evening dew forms,
The night begins crying,
Sensitive, Night Rose,
To the impatient waiting,
Caught, Passion Rose,
By the sensuous rhythm
Of a petal falling
And a fantasy's frantic calling.

One Day At A Time

In the distant near, helpless,
Waits your fantasy, Night Rose
And like crystal moonlight, Passion Rose
Touches lightly your thorns exposed,
Gently crying,
Then sighs softly,
As your petal lands unbroken and the fantasy waits.

Simply A Note to Ask
(17 July 2008, Q. Hill)

Simply a note to ask,
When did yesterday become brighter than today,
Or, the million sad tomorrows?

When did kisses blown in the wind,
Hold more love than the ones missed?
When did loveless nights replace ecstasy released?
And love received becomes a box of empty space?

What of the promise given that day
When joy in celebration tears first past,
And your beauty unsurpassed tore my heart away?

Drowning in love all passed sorrows,
Each breath of you tattooing my mind,
Still my lips remember when we kissed,
My body, the joyous climatic feast,
When our need neon-lit our face,
Were those lies spoken in that place?

Simply a note to ask,
When did we lose that day?

Reflections

When true love happens, it does not ask permission or allow any discussion. Love simply is, and that's more than enough to overwhelm all of you. The thing is Love doesn't always happen in pairs. Sometimes one half falls deeply into it and the other simple doesn't. Love does not care.

Notes and Insights

One Day At A Time

Session 14

PRAISE, SIMPLE PRAISE

We are in a time where our faith is subject to assaults of all kinds, and we are sustained because our Lord and Savior Lives. We are under undue pressure at all times and from sometimes unknown directions, but our everyday life is made special by the pardon purchased for us by our Savior. The love we have for each other is a portion of the share given us by the Sacrifice on the Cross and because our Savior stayed there for us. We are blessed in ways we cannot count not because of what is said, or what we know, or what we do, but as a result of the Faith of Jesus when He trusted that His Father our God would raise Him from the dead. We are alive, able to praise, to worship, and to rest in the arms of our Lord because the truth of it all is that He Lives!

I believe we are each written into the Word of God. Woven into the fabric of the words and phrases, shown in the lives lived there, and covered by the Grace and Mercy shown there. Even though every Word is true and applicable to our lives, we are usually drawn to particular scriptures, passages of words or verses. There is a magnetic call felt when our eyes and hearts take in certain words of Biblical Word. Words that speak to our deepest places, and give us complete peace. Mine is Psalms

116. The whole Session, each word speaks truth into me, lifts me when I am lost or down, and reminds me of the price paid by Jesus and the unpayable debt of His sacrifice. It also comforts me, and we each at one time or another need the comfort beyond measure. If you believe or not and do not have a bit of the Word you know that speaks directly to you, then you have not looked. The Word is such that even a casual reading will point you to what is needed. Some of my verses are:

> [5] The Lord is gracious and righteous; our God is full of compassion.
> [6] The Lord protects the unwary; when I was brought low, he saved me.
> [7] Return to your rest, my soul, for the Lord has been good to you.
>
> Psalms 116: 5-7

PRAISE, SIMPLE PRAISE

The Only I AM!
(26 September 2006, Q. Hill)

Dawn crashes through my dreams,
Awakening me to the call of the day.
Praises burst, unbidden, from my spirit,
Rushing outward, flying, raising, seeking,
Calling, beckoning, singing for me to join.

Crushed down in raising praises,
Shaking with need,
Crying from the restraints, bindings,
My spirit, Alone, just me, just you, Freed.

All boundaries, broken, the Naked Cross,
My soul, my spirit explodes, multicolored,
Celebrating, again, the rebirth of joy,
Touching, briefly, the essence, your spirit,
Rejoicing, in the song, the symphony, the worship.

As everything celebrates,
Hallelujah, Hallelujah,
Hallelujah, The only I AM.
Praises, unrestrained, exposed and revealed,
Celebrating, worshiping, the only I AM, my God.

One Day At A Time

Slowly, stumbling, refreshed, released,
As dawn crashes through my dreams,
Another day begins as the night ends,
Praises bubble, bursting, from my spirit,
Celebrating, over and over, the only I AM, my God!!

Who Touched Me?
(10 October 2005, Q. Hill)

Every tear flowed without ceasing,
Washing hopes, dreams, like used tissue, away,
Leaving emptiness injured, hurt, life seeking.
Hopeless, broke, broken, just the grave, waiting,
Slowly filled with yesterdays, tomorrows, mine,
Drowning my todays leaving me faint, falling.
Then He brushed me, just a caress.
Suddenly, lighter than a feather,
Dreams, mine, float by me, rising, pirouetting,
Dancing, embraced by Hopes long lost, blessed.
Shedding yesterday's darkness, laughter appeared,
Still, my tears flowed without ceasing.
Again. He touched me, just a breath of air.
Light filled, love healed, still I seek,
Who touched me?
Washing my yesterdays, lifting my joy,
Who touched me?
Barely a caress, so gentle it seems, but what power.
Who touched me?
Gold has no value, so priceless this seems.
Who touched me?
Please touch me, touch me, love me again!

Still You

(05 January 2021, Q. Hill)

The everyday risks of falling short attack me,
Causing my shame to grow and grow,
Leaving me with sore knees and no results,
My every effort fails, breaking my will,
And again I fall to the temptations, sin overcomes,
Still He doesn't forsake or release me.

My wilderness moments increase tear by tear,
Drowning my resistance, overflowing my cup,
Not with blessings, mercy or Your Grace,
No, flooding my beliefs with doubts,
Causing my shame to grow and grow,
Still Your Presence calls to me.

When last I prayed my words seemed hollow,
Echoing in my head, shattering my peace,
I repeat words taught in Sunday school,
Our Father, Hoping this time they will be heard, received,
And, not fall again as dead leaves, killed by my shame,
Still You listened then comforted me.

Praise, Simple Praise

Last night I awakened, tears washing my soul,
In desperation and shame, I called out, Help me,
The silence of no answer assaulted the waiting space,
And the tears became a flood, cries of a child lost,
Gasping, I sought safety in a bottle and a dream,
Still You forgave and welcomed me.

In my moment of extreme need, I bowed, broken,
My soul wounded, my body weakened, my spirit stripped,
Yet, unable to see, there is no light, I seek peace,
My cries rise, tearing through the darkening sky,
Carrying my grief, my pain, my need, my name,
And, in the quiet Still, you Loved me.

And I Live

(20 October 2011, Q. Hill)

Redeemed by the Word,
Caught in my sin, I cried,
Broken by the loss, Dreams, faded,
Unable to find Hope, I fell,
Bruised and beaten, tomorrow, out of reach,
Still the Redeemer calls,
And I live, Forgiven.

Cross held, pierced and Bled,
Everyday struggling, failing, crying,
No successes, no victories, Dreams Fading,
Lost in today, into tomorrow, I fall,
Fighting, losing, unable to answer the door,
Still the Redeemer knocks,
And I live, Blood washed.

Resurrected, 3 days of Love's Sacrifice,
Releasing today, yesterday, I worshiped,
Found, no longer Dreaming, I am lifted,
Words become prayers, Hope lives,
Wounded, still hurting, now healed,
believing, Still the Redeemer lives,
And I died, now for Him I live.

Galatians 2:20:

"I have been crucified **with Christ** and I no longer **live**, but **Christ live**s in me. The life I now **live** in the body, I **live** by faith in the Son of God, who loved me and gave himself for me."

One Day At A Time

Deity and Sacrifice

We live in a world, where gods are made, changed, and destroyed at the whim of the latest crave or personal desire. We stand out as different or out of date or simply uninformed by most of those who bother to have an opinion of us and our faith. Because of our faith, and because our Lord and Savior Lives, we are under undue pressure, often from unknown directions. Our every day is made special by the pardon purchased for us by our Savior. The love we have for each other is a portion of the share given us by the Sacrifice on the Cross and because our Savior stayed there on the cross for us. We are blessed in ways we cannot count not because of what is said, or what we know, or what we do, but as a result of the Faith of Jesus when He trusted that His Father our God would raise Him from the dead. We are alive, able to praise, to worship, and to rest in the arms of our Lord because the truth of it all is that He Lives!

When speaking of deity and the sacrifice, we must first define what we are talking about. For this conversation, deity is defined by the sacrifice. In defining sacrifice for this conversation, there is a need to frame it in a manner that can be understood in human terms. Sacrifice is often thought of as giving up or letting go of something extremely important to us. But, for this conversation we must go beyond that to what sacrifice means if you are a deity of the highest order. Christ exemplified sacrifice at this level on the cross. He trusted His deity to His Father, the Lord God, and because of that He Lives.

Praise, Simple Praise

To understand the nature and depth of the price paid for our redemption as part of defining deity, there is a need to view the happenings on the cross differently, from the aspect, in as much as is possible, of the one who hung there and died. Imagine standing on the shore of a great ocean, staring out to the horizon and seeing it become hazy and unclear. Standing staring into the unknown but knowing the ocean exists and goes on beyond your ability to see, feel, or comprehend. Are you there yet, can you see the forever that is illustrated, the longing for knowledge of the parts beyond your ability to see? Now imagine you have seen and experienced the forever and know the depth of the ocean separating you from it. Add to that your home, your family; the center of your love is there beyond the horizon. Sacrifice is giving all that up knowing that the forever you are a part of ends. There is nothing beyond the edge of the horizon.

Compare it to an egg being rolled across a high table. And as the edge of the table nears, the egg knows if it goes over the edge, there is no coming back. It will be broken beyond recovery. Imagine also that the egg has the ability to stop and not go over the edge. All it has to do is choose to stop. All Christ had to do was choose to come down from the cross. But, because He chose to stay, we live because He Lives.

The illustration above is an attempt to bring into focus the nature of sacrifice when the choice is forever and beyond or simply ending. Not just an ending of you, but of all the things, happenings, the sacrifice of others and most importantly, the future of untold generations. Consider the weight of the choice. This is part of what it means to be deity. But not just any deity, because people have always made deities of common, unknown, or favored things, or have used might to make deities, forcing those weaker to bow to what they believe. Not a deity of yours or my imagination that fits into our human understanding or our ability to explain. Yes, I know this piece appears just that, an attempt to explain deity by using sacrifice as a point of reference.

In the Midst of Sadness
(10 November 2006, Q. Hill)

In the midst of sadness,
You forgot, turned left,
Joy fled seeking your refuge,
On a fence, sitting, your words unkept,
Unfaithfulness causes the broken gladness,
And then, alone, me, you.

Left to last, before you began,
Tears, swell, waves, despair overflow, me,
Reaching for rescue, for you, left drifting,
Sadness covers my fears, shifting, as sand,
Calling you, not me, gladness flees.

My Lord, the cross, lifting,
In the midst of sadness, words unkept,
Salvation, not free, no price quote,
Paid, no balance outstanding,
Savior, me, an open hand,
My life, hidden sins, you, sifting,
Still open, beckoning, my tears fell.

One Day At A Time

January One, new year's begun,
But, it is Summer, Spring,
And from East to West, Run,
Changing, fearing, joy within sings,
The cross empty, the purchase, me,
The hand, a cloth, my tears, cleansing,
In the midst of sadness, promises kept,
And then, no longer alone, me, you, free.

Praise, Simple Praise

It Only Matters
(16 April 2013, Q. Hill)

It doesn't matter the day or time,
The offense, real or imagine, or the crime,
It doesn't matter the wishes or greatest hope,
The planned or handed down dreams,
It doesn't matter if it was intended to be,
Or if just by chance surprising and free,
It does matter the words spoken
In truth, or as lies, or just as a token,
It doesn't matter who loved you,
Or who you loved, none were so true,
It doesn't matter the tears shed,
Or the life you've led,
It only matters what He said,
His Blood for you freely bled,
There is no hiding from what is true,
Love is all that, cross-held, saved you
It only matters that for your life,
The whip scourged Him with stripes,
It only matters for you He died,
And for you, He did Rise,
It doesn't matter if you believe,
Your sins He did relieve,
It only matters that He gave,
And because Him you are Saved.

Don't Play
(09/14/2010, q. hill)

Ain't got no more patience,
No more time to wait,
On you, on Jesus, on God
Got no more time to waste
No more dollars and cents
Not another issue can I take.
Stop; don't speak of your Lord,
It is just too damn late,
Plus that, life don't play.

Church house, filled with lies and flies,
The good ones covered by the smell,
The stink of those just gaming, playing,
You, me, but I'm done with all that
God knows my efforts, my tries,
Preacher, took my secrets to sell,
Caring, not for me, only those paying
Not going to church to get jacked,
That's life and life don't play.

Praise, Simple Praise

Why praise, why worship, why care,
The Cross, His Life Given, so what,
I see what I see, hear what is truly said,
I'm broken, where is a place for me
You have no time, no love to spare,
I do what I must, no If, and, or But,
God knows, my tears, my soul has bled,
He's seen my sins, the horrors I flee,
His Life, for me, please, don't play.

Notes and Insights

Praise, Simple Praise

Session 15

SESSION IN PRAYER – IN PRAYER WITH YOU

Each day should begin and end in prayer. For me it is simple: we are called to give homage to the Creator of all things, including us. This is not a discussion of mine or your deity, or of your god versus mine, or of how the world and you or I came to be. Not at all, I leave that to people smarter and more devout than me. This is about acknowledging there is something greater than each of us. Greater than all our discoveries, all our accomplishments, greater than all we can think or imagine. It may not be as simple for you, and that is alright. But, for me and my house, we serve the Lord, our God and do so without reservation.

Prayer comes in many forms. It is not so much how you pray, although many signature books of worship do give instructions on the manner and content of our prayers, but it is important you pray. Session in prayer should happen at least when you begin your day and when you end your day. This is simple respect and honor. You will find as you go about living there are numerous opportunities or occasions to pray. Sometimes it is to give thanks, respect, and honor. Other times it is to acknowledge a gift given, or trouble avoided, or a difficulty overcome.

There are times when an event or occurrence causes you to pray and pray with all your being. Times like when my daughter was having a pain crisis, and all the doctors could do was not enough to heal her, was not enough to stop the pain for very long or stop the ravages the disease was having on her body, was not enough to stop her cries and moans. Those are times when you must pray, and pray with your whole being, even though you may hide your tears from your loved one, you must pray. The need to pray can happen at any time, under any circumstances.

SESSION IN PRAYER – IN PRAYER WITH YOU

Why Just Pray?
(04 February 2021, Q. Hill)

Is there a place?
A place for my tears often shed in anger,
A place for my pain, slowly ripping me apart,
A place for love, mine left me, alone I am.
Why pray?

Are there words I can speak?
For the broken parts of me,
That fills my empty heart,
And, slows my life, today it was a blur.
Why pray?

Is anything or anyone listening?
To the everyday needs calling me,
To the people shouting and harming me,
To the nightmares stealing my sleep and my peace?
Why pray?

Is there one who understands?
The cries of a broken man,
The needs of a lost daughter or son,
Listening to whispers of an abused wife?
Why pray?

One Day At A Time

Is there truth in the words just pray?
When yesterday becomes today,
And tomorrow becomes yesterday,
But, the answer is still so far away.
Why pray?

Why just pray?
There is power in the words,
There is life in your belief,
The answer is the Lord's,
And, just beyond your prayer.

SESSION IN PRAYER – IN PRAYER WITH YOU

My Prayers Include You
(08 February 2021, Q. Hill)

My morning prayers always include you,
No matter the day or circumstances,
The prayers always include you.
Sometimes the heart is broken,
Hurt by the passage of the day before,
Bruised by words spoken and unspoken,
Lost seeking love lost and renewed,
And, each day my morning prayers include you.

My midday prayers always include you,
No matter the events good or bad that are occurring,
The prayers always include you.
Sometimes my heart seeks a token,
Hurt by the actions of others, you, and unable to ignore,
Bruised by the day, in pain since awoken,
Lost, I am seeking a path for love to come through,
And, each day my midday prayers include you.

One Day At A Time

My evening prayers always include you,
No matter the joys, celebrations, or regrets of the day,
The prayers always include you.
Sometimes as the evening breaks, my heart is broken,
Hurt by the success and failures, each waves on the seashore,
Bruised by the pounding surf, drifting and broken,
Lost, as each wave washed my love, the love of you,
And, each day my evening prayers include you.

Session in Prayer – In Prayer with You

Such A Beautiful Day!
(06 October 2005, Q. Hill)

Did you ever wonder?
Why God loves you so much,
Why He chose you for this life,
Why Jesus gave His all for you?

Did you cry when you realized,
That it was not just for you,
Not because of what was asked,
Not because of who you are,
Or because of what you do?

It is such a beautiful day,
Today, the first of tomorrow,
The last of yesterday,
Today is such a beautiful gift.

Last night you may have cried,
Yesterday you may have lied,
Before you may have hurt and victimized,
Everywhere was pain, your shame.

One Day At A Time

But, it is still a beautiful day, today,
Such a beautiful gift!
You are forgiven,
He blesses our every way,
You are so precious to Him.

Did you ever wonder?

Why God loves you so much,
Why Jesus stayed on the cross,
Does it make you cry?
Well, what of me,
God shares Himself with me,
What a joyous gift,
His Love for us!

No fireworks, or balloons floating free,
No parades, or big TO DOs,
No grand speeches or awards,
But, what a celebration, joy released,
Such a beautiful day,
Such a precious gift!

Celebrate, Celebrate, Celebrate!
Such a beautiful day!

Notes and Insights

One Day At A Time

Session 16

ONE LAST THING

As you live every day, you find yourself farther from the times and places you live within your mind. These places carry more than your yesterdays; they also remind you of the choices made, some yours, some others, some out of your control. These choices have left marks, scars, on your everyday, scars that stand out calling to your soul crying for peace. Places and the choices related to the marks are often the only roadmap you have to portions of your life lived out loud. And as we move through time and away from the places and the time where it may have happened, the mind often heals by lessening the impact, the brightness, and the sharpness of the joy, sadness, or pain felt. And like a paper map, the images recalled are only in two dimensions lacking the depth and reality necessary for the instances to be real. You know what happened, not always why it happened, but you know it happened. Like with PTSD, the dreams are real and often so are your screams and tears.

What is this rambling all about, regrets, dreams, losses, wins, or things imagined? It depends is the only answer that covers the times and places past. It is about the words. Words are used to paint the pictures, recreate the images, and create new pictures. Often the images are hidden within the many metaphors life creates. Metaphors are the phases opening one mind to another allowing the listener to enter the kaleidoscope landscape of the speaker's mind. Sometimes the words speak plainly. Like the ones below.

As the night covers the day, or the sunlight renews the joys of living, so does love in its many shades from bright to deepest blue, from unbelievably intense to gently cradling your heart, to carrying the weight of extreme lost and the emptiness that comes with it, Love does it all and so much more. So, why is it so hard to love completely?

Peace is the quietness before a storm, the gentle smoothness on the surface of an ocean, miles deep, and the embrace of love wrapping you in the forever warmth which covers no matter what is happening.

Life is lived in sessions, with each session lived on its own, but like metaphors, the truth of life lived out loud is often hidden in the words and phrases telling the story. Peace.

Psalm 116

> [1] I love the LORD, for He heard my voice;
> He heard my cry for mercy.
> [2] Because He turned His ear to me,
> I will call on Him as long as I live.
> Praise the LORD.

This manuscript was complete, at least I thought it was, and then God whispered, "What of the heartache? The pain you bring to each other. What of that?" Stopped by the words whispering in my ear, I tried to recall all the times this pain was spoken of in this manuscript. I tried to recall each word, each phrase of prose, lines written to bring to life the pain of just living. The whisper returned, saying a single word, "Love." "Love" is spoken of here, time and time again. Love of life, love of another, love of God. What more is there to say about Love, losing it? I spoke of that also, and in great detail. Then the whisper said, "Release your heart to speak of it."

Now, shocked by the tears that suddenly flood my soul and pain released, I write these words:

Love for the heart is Life, and no matter how long or how many you love, Love is sharp on both edges. One edge that opens you to a place within Love beyond measure, and the other, sometimes sharp, other times very dull, cuts from you Love leaving wounds so deep there is no cure for the pain, no medicine, or remedy. But Life goes on because Life is a Gift from God who is Love. And even with your wounds, your brokenness, your unbelievable loneliness, God continues to Love you and give another chance, another opportunity to love as you are designed. He does not take away the pain of loss, or hurt of love leaving you for another, or the loneliness of waking to find the place where love resided empty. He fills them with Himself, overflowing and covering all the lost, all the hurt, all the loneliness, and opening you to living the Life He has given you. Love is sharp on both edges, and God Heals both cuts.

Is this what hasn't been included here? I don't think so. There are pieces and narratives about love and God's Gift of it. Have we spoken of Forgiveness, that's part God's Love. Yes. Have we spoken of the joy of waking every day, that's part of God's Love. Yes. Have we spoken of the endless river of tears, crystal and broken, that have fallen only to be caught by the Love of God? Yes. Have we described with words inadequate for the job, Love's beauty and joy, Love's carrying us to flights of fantasy and ecstasy with unbelievable release, that's part of God's Love. And, being able to pray and rest in peace in the Glory of the God above all else, is that not love beyond measure and haven't we spoken of that?

Is that God's Love is endless and is with us no matter what, where or when we are? But, didn't we speak of that. Therein is the problem, these words, or for that matter any words, are inadequate to describe or illustrate the smallest portion of God's Love. We try and know our efforts fall short, and it is alright because God Loves us. And, God's Love is all you need. Is this what God is whispering for us to hear and live?

One Last Thing

Silent Daze, Silent Days
(27 January 2022, Q. Hill)

Our silent gaze, unable to look away,
Shows us, reveals us, hides us, and,
We turn lost in the dream smoke, drifting,
Simply clouds, torn and blown by the wind,
Content, satisfied with, accepting it, today,
Lies, untruths, whispers, shouts, and,
Words spoken, unmeant, soul lifting,
Causing our silent gaze, lost we stand,
In the echo of our silent daze, our silent days,
Looking to others, our new gods.

Our silent daze, staring into nothing, unblinking,
Looking for forever, searching for yesterday, and,
Lost we turn, drifting, smother by the dream smoke,
Blown by the wind, the clouds, you, break and tatter,
But, content, satisfied and accepting, deep breathing,
We breath the lies, untruths, repeat whispers, and,
Shout words, soul lifting, unmeant, dream smoke,
Lost to our silent daze, living silent days that no longer matter,
Crying for our new gods, expecting God to answer.

One Day At A Time

Our silent days, follow one another, forever,
Reflecting nothing, revealing us, hiding us, and,
Standing, we no longer move, dream smoke, smothers,
Unmoved by the winds, our clouds, blown away,
As contentedly, deep breathing, in the stormy weather
We believe the lies, untruths, shout the whispers, and,
While tears drop, soul breaking, no sister or brother,
Strong, unmovable, holding us, having the last say,
As our God waits, just beyond our silent daze, silent days.

ABOUT THE AUTHOR

Quinn Hill was born during the Forgotten War, the Korean Conflict, as a child without a father who was delivered into the loving arms of Big Mama. Often referred to as the "he will be alright" kid, he lived and survived on the streets of many cities including San Antonio, Dallas, Las Vegas, Los Angeles, and Detroit. Living the struggle of painfully poor, books or anything with print became Quinn's refuge. This love of reading and the freedom it gives prepared him to be a winner at life on the streets and for entering college at an early age.

When his draft number came up during the Vietnam War, Quinn chose the United States Air Force as a means of escaping the meat grinder and horror of a losing war. Enlisting for the short tour, he volunteered for special duty service, working on highly classified systems and missions around the world. His tours of duty took him to numerous countries across the globe, some of those countries no longer exist having been conquered or absolved. Quinn survived the turmoil and trauma of his military service by writing, which allowed him to capture the beauty, joy, and pain of a life lived out loud. But still he was unable to avoid the reality of life lived according to someone else's rules.

One Day At A Time

His military career lasted 26 years and was followed by careers in engineering, finance, information technology, and cybersecurity. Now retired, Quinn enjoys family, reading, and writing and has sprinkled in gardening, travel, golf, and working with others. Learning to live life one day at a time was a process, one Quinn learned by seeing life in its many forms flavored by the many cultures he experienced.

Believing that every life has merit, Quinn spends time working with young people from hard and often dangerous neighborhoods. He has been a nationwide speaker at youth and young adult conferences. Quinn often speaks with young people, teachers, law enforcement, and social services about intervention strategies, mentoring, and healing. His efforts are geared toward equipping young people for whatever they are going to create. Blessed with a voice and a belief driven by faith, Quinn believes every day is a journey that can only be lived one day at a time.

Warrior, father, brother, friend, and man of faith, Quinn has seen most of the world and lived a life full of grace.

A Letter to You

Baba,

I'm so proud of you. This work of art, everything you've been through, and being able to pull yourself up and make a life for yourself - it's admirable. Thank you for allowing me to help you edit something so special to you and be a part of your journey. I wish you nothing but success, even if you don't publish it (but, I hope you do). The world needs your wisdom and love, and hopefully this hard coy inspires that.

I'm so grateful to know you and call you my Baba. You're the coolest person I know.

I love you.

Your Road-Dog, Jasmine

AFTERWORDS

Josiah, named for a King, simply my grandson. Josiah, King, a star seeking its place among the heavenly host, and a star shining uncontrollably bright here amongst us. Josiah, lover of the ostracized, the ones picked on for being different, the ones needing a voice and star. Josiah; son, brother, friend, and simply loved by all who met him and shared just one moment. Josiah, whose life runway was simply not long enough, and he chose to take flight before reaching its end. Josiah, a million, million tears are not enough to speak my love for you. We each have our journey; I will look for you as I walk mine. Peace.

Josiah, King

(q.hill, 03/16/23)

Speaking into tomorrow
Wanting all to hear, style
Creating images, drawn in love
In a world gone crazy, lost,

One Day At A Time

Breaking life's flow, simply free
With expressions, some high, some low,
Sung by a choir, love's simple melody
Given freely, such a high cost, peace.

Ebony sounds, echoing images
Reflecting forever, one tear at a time,
Falling on the brokenness, you, me,
Recalling yesterday, setting you free, fly,
Inspiring designs, expanding creative edges,
Drawn by you, your smile, mine,
Speaking love, on a rose-colored sea,
Whispering, please don't cry,
For today, I am flying free.

Speaking love into today,
Not of yesterday's pains,
Or, even of tomorrow's hopes,
Mine for you include everything,
So, please smile as you see,
See again, and again, the angel,
The angel that is me,
Resting with our Lord, simply free

CPSIA information can be obtained
at www.ICGtesting.com
Printed in the USA
JSHW010944250523
42234JS00003B/4